From Pirates to Drug Lords

SUNY Series in Global Politics
James N. Rosenau, Editor

From Pirates to Drug Lords

The Post–Cold War Caribbean
Security Environment

EDITED BY
Michael C. Desch,
Jorge I. Domínguez, and
Andrés Serbin

STATE UNIVERSITY OF NEW YORK PRESS

Published by
State University of New York Press, Albany

© 1998 State University of New York

For information, address State University of New York Press,
State University Plaza, Albany, N.Y., 12246

Production by Cathleen Collins
Marketing by Fran Keneston

Library of Congress Cataloging in Publication Data

From pirates to drug lords : the Post-Cold War Caribbean security
    environment / edited by Michael C. Desch, Jorge I. Domínguez, and
    Andrés Serbin.
        p.   cm. — (SUNY series in global politics)
    Includes bibliographical references and index.
    Contents: Hurricanes are not the only intruders : the Caribbean in
    an era of global turbulence / James N. Rosenau — The state of the
    region / Anthony T. Bryan — Globalization, regionalization and
    Civil Society in the Greater Caribbean / Andrés Serbin — The
    powers, the pirates, and international norms and institutions in the
    American Mediterranean / Jorge I. Domínguez — The geography
    of drug trafficking in the Caribbean / Ivelaw L. Griffith — Security
    in the greater Caribbean : what role for collective security mechanisms?
    / Richard Bloomfield — New issues Regional on the security agenda
    for the Caribbean : drugs, environment, migration, and democratic
    stability / Instituto de Altos Estudios de la Defensa Nacional, Venezuela.
        ISBN 0-7914-3749-3 (hardcover : alk. paper). — ISBN 0-7914-3750-7
    (pbk. : alk. paper)
        1. Caribbean Area—Politics and government—1945-   2. Caribbean
    Area—Social conditions.   3. Caribbean Area—Economic conditions.
    4. National security—Caribbean Area.   I. Desch, Michael C.
    (Michael Charles), 1960-   . II. Domínguez, Jorge I., 1945-   .
    III. Serbin, Andrés.   IV. Series.
    F2183.F76   1998
    972.905—dc21   97-23334
                                                              CIP

10 9 8 7 6 5 4 3 2 1

Contents

Preface
MICHAEL C. DESCH   vii

1   Introduction
    JORGE I. DOMÍNGUEZ   1

2   Hurricanes Are Not the Only Intruders
    The Caribbean in an Era of Global Turbulence
    JAMES N. ROSENAU   11

3   The State of the Region
    Trends Affecting the Future of Caribbean Security
    ANTHONY T. BRYAN   33

4   Globalization, Regionalization, and Civil Society
    in the Greater Caribbean
    ANDRÉS SERBIN   55

5   The Powers, the Pirates, and International Norms
    and Institutions in the American Mediterranean
    JORGE I. DOMÍNGUEZ   79

6   The Geography of Drug Trafficking in the Caribbean
    IVELAW L. GRIFFITH   97

7   Security in the Greater Caribbean
    What Role for Collective Security Mechanisms?
    RICHARD J. BLOOMFIELD   121

8   New Issues on the Regional Security Agenda for the Caribbean
    Drugs, Environment, Migration, and Democratic Stability
    INSTITUTO DE ALTOS ESTUDIOS DE LA DEFENSA NACIONAL, VENEZUELA   133

9   Conclusion
    MICHAEL C. DESCH   145

    About the Contributors   155

    Index   157

Preface

MICHAEL C. DESCH

With the end of the Cold War, the strategic importance of the Western Hemisphere and the Caribbean Basin has diminished significantly for most of the extra-regional actors traditionally involved in the area. At the same time, for most of the regional actors, threat perceptions, security priorities, and even traditional definitions of national security have changed. Diverging threat perceptions and different security priorities have converged with an increasing regional awareness of the need to advance the regionalization process through collective mechanisms such as the recently established Association of Caribbean States to create a complex and diversified security environment in the Caribbean Basin. However, most of the subregional integration initiatives, while addressing economic cooperation and trade liberalization, do not address security issues. In fact, these issues are systematically avoided in most of the current subregional agreements, notwithstanding the fact that most of them strongly rely on previous political and diplomatic initiatives.

This new situation raises some important questions regarding the primary threat perceptions in the region and their relation to new issues on the international agenda, such as trade liberalization, economic integration, migration, narcotics trafficking, and environmental degradation. These new issues, in turn, must be related to the legacies of the older security agenda, which includes some unresolved boundary and territorial disputes, continuing conflicts over maritime jurisdictional limits, and the persistence of the Cold War in U. S.–Cuban relations.

These questions sparked two related conferences that were jointly sponsored by the John M. Olin Institute for Strategic Studies, the David

Rockefeller Center for Latin American Studies, the Center for International Affairs of Harvard University, the North-South Center of the University of Miami, the Fundacion Gran Mariscal de Ayacucho, and the Instituto Venezolano de Estudios Sociales y Politicos of Caracas, Venezuela.

In late November 1993, the first conference, "Global Change and Hemispheric Security," was held at the Harvard University Faculty Club. Top Latin American and military leaders, joined by prominent academics and policy makers, sat down together to discuss "Global Change and Hemispheric Security." Topics included "Change in the Global Environment and Its Impact on Hemispheric Security," "New Security Challenges in the Interamerican System," "Democratic Government and Future Patterns of Civil-Military Relations in the Western Hemisphere," and "New Elements on the Future Hemispheric Security Agenda." Among those in attendance were many prominent North American and Latin American academics and former and current policy makers, including Ambassador Luigi Einaudi, one of the State Department's key architects of U. S. Latin American policy.

In October 1995, a second workshop, "International Security in the Greater Caribbean," was held at the Center for International Affairs. The primary aim of the workshop was to discuss the dominant threat perceptions and security priorities of regional governments, the varied mechanisms that were in place to promote regional collective action, and the future agenda of U. S. foreign policy toward the Caribbean, especially in terms of Haiti and Cuba. The chapters in this volume represent the results of this second workshop.

In addition to the authors and commentators involved with the second conference, we would like to thank Professor Samuel P. Huntington, director of the John M. Olin Institute for Strategic Studies, and Professor John Coatsworth, director of the David Rockefeller Center for Latin American Studies, both of Harvard University, for institutional support of both of these intellectual efforts to think about how the end of the Cold War has affected hemispheric security affairs. We also gratefully acknowledge the efforts of Inga Peterson, Carol Edwards, John Stephenson, and Chung Lee in the production of this book.

1

INTRODUCTION

JORGE I. DOMÍNGUEZ

Within days of the collapse of the Berlin wall, marking the end of the Cold War in Europe, in December 1989 the U. S. armed forces intervened massively and unilaterally in Panama to overthrow its government. These twinned events call attention to the themes of continuity and change at the same moment in international history and remind us of the persistence of U. S. military intervention in the greater Caribbean region across time and circumstances.

In the recent past, the United States also intervened in Grenada in 1983 and in Haiti in 1994. Compared to the intervention in Panama, these two other interventions call attention to a third theme in the region's history: under specific circumstances, other governments are prepared to join the United States to intervene militarily in the internal affairs of a neighboring country to advance goals they hold dear. In Grenada, U. S. forces were joined by those from Jamaica, Barbados, Dominica, St. Vincent and the Grenadines, St. Lucia, and Antigua; in Haiti, the United States acted under the authorization of the United Nations Security Council. Collective military action came to play a significant role in the Caribbean at the end of the twentieth century.

The Caribbean has hosted some of the most decisive confrontations in the history of the United States as a world power. The United States had to secure the region for the safe passage of its ships during World War I and World War II to enable the successful deployment of U. S. forces to defeat Germany's military might. And, in 1962, the United States and the Soviet Union came closer to a nuclear confrontation than at any other time since nuclear bombs had been dropped on Japan in 1945.

The Caribbean, in short, is very much a part of the history of international security in our times, as it has been through centuries past. But the question of Caribbean security matters, above all, to its own people, who have been fought over and invaded by major powers since a small Spanish flotilla blundered into its waters in 1492. Even as the millennium comes to a close, the legacies of centuries of colonial rule remain evident in the Caribbean, where several island countries remain formal dependencies of the United Kingdom, France, the Netherlands, and the United States.

The Caribbean's insecurities, today, as in centuries past, stem from far more than the confrontations amidst the major powers, however. Among governments, there remain serious boundary issues that have occasionally threatened to become reasons for war. The Dominican Republic and Haiti, Venezuela and Guyana, and Nicaragua and Colombia exemplify classic and still unresolved ancient interstate border disputes. In the Caribbean, serious military events have occurred at various times pertaining to Cuba. Cuba was at the heart of the U. S.–Soviet struggle in 1962, and it was the object of a U. S.–sponsored exile invasion in 1961; U. S. and Cuban forces fought each other on Grenadan soil in 1983; and Cuba sank a Bahamian Coast Guard ship in international waters in 1980 and shot down two unarmed civilian aircraft, also over international waters, in 1996.

The most common sources of insecurity in the Caribbean affect the quotidian experiences of ordinary people. The societies of most Caribbean countries are deeply affected by the spread of transnational crime, directly connected to the boom in illegal drug consumption in the United States since the late 1960s. Caribbean countries are ideally located on the transit routes of cocaine traffickers from the producing centers in South America. The spread of violence related to drug trafficking threatens to overwhelm the governments of the smaller islands and undermine and corrupt the governments of all of the islands.

Suppose, however, that we limit the word *security* to instances that involve the deliberate use of force for allegedly rational ends. This would include the 1962 Cuban missile crisis, as well as the violent actions of drug traffickers in the same broad category. There are, nonetheless, many other sources of insecurity in the Caribbean, as seen by governments and individuals in the region.

Hundreds of thousands of people from the islands migrate illegally to some other country every year; many are caught and turned back, others drown, but many others make the journey successfully. Such migration poses starkly the incapacity of governments to control their borders and the grave risk to the safety of those who seek to make the journey. The Caribbean suffers also from severe environmental problems. Deforestation and land erosion in Haiti, for example, threaten the livelihood and survival of an entire country, motivating pressures for emigration as a result. And Caribbean peoples are regularly victims of natural disasters, such as hurricanes, volcanoes, and earthquakes.

In this book, we will explore the connection between security themes, narrowly defined, and a panoply of processes, events, and circumstances that enrich our understanding of the conditions of this region and its people. It may be worth it to identify some of these overarching concerns that go beyond security issues.

THE OLD AND THE NEW

The Economy

Since the late fifteenth century, the Caribbean has been deeply integrated in the world economy. The concept of the "globalization" of the economy is often cited as a late twentieth-century phenomenon, but it has been an essential concern of life, work, and production in the Caribbean for over half a millennium. In the Caribbean, moreover, such globalization has always gone hand in hand with production specialization—as true of the sugar plantations of old as of the Club Med tourist enclaves today.

The principal shift in recent times in the Caribbean's political economy stems from the retreat of the world's major powers in their commitment to shield in some fashion the economies of the Caribbean from the gale winds of international market forces. The North American Free Trade Agreement (NAFTA), which went into effect on January 1, 1994, groups the United States, Canada, and Mexico; it greatly reduces the worth of U. S. and Canadian trade preferences for Caribbean countries codified in the Caribbean Basin Initiative (CBI) and the Canadian-Caribbean Agreement (CARIBCAN), respectively. Similarly, the European Union's Lomé Convention trade preferences for Caribbean bananas have been under sustained and increasingly effective attack by a coalition that has included the United States and other governments and firms, many within the European Union (EU). The Soviet Union collapsed, and with it disappeared its erstwhile subsidies to Cuba. In short, the Caribbean's economy, always globalized, is today more internationally vulnerable.

The Caribbean has been an arena for the practical application of new technologies and for business innovation. Damnable as it was in its devastating effects on human beings, the Caribbean's slave-based agricultural plantations were once models of international competitive efficiency. But

also at mid-millennium, the Caribbean was the site of impressive technological improvements in navigation and naval warfare. In the early twentieth century, its people built and Panama hosted a new interoceanic canal.
And in the 1950s, Fidel Castro demonstrated how to make a revolution on
television, in a country wired helpfully for sound and image.

In the 1990s, financial specialization, electronic banking, and innovative design of financial regulations have generated spectacular growth on
many of the islands; this strategy has long been of critical importance to
Panama's development. Though most of these have been lawful activities,
they have also incubated international money laundering. Efficient law-
abiding firms continue to coexist with illegal ones in the Caribbean, however, today, all are principally in the service sector.

Environment and Health

Scholars of international relations at times refer to a new international
agenda, the environment most prominently on it. Yet concerns about the
environment have always been part of the region's very being. Caribbean
peoples know with utter certainty that hurricanes will arrive in the summer and autumn every year, though they never know the exact moment
when these monsters will strike. The damage from these events has been
incalculable.

Today, there are additional concerns about the environment. The extent of soil erosion on some of the islands is alarming. The potential effects
of global warming as a result of changes in the world's climate gravely
threaten small islands. At the minimum, the beaches that are essential for
tourism may be washed away; at the worst, an entire country could disap-
pear. For some Caribbean islands, consequently, changes in global climate
are as important as the effects of nuclear war. The rise in international concern about the environment has also injected many new actors into the
Caribbean, principally nongovernmental organizations (NGOs) with specific causes to advance.

The Caribbean, moreover, was founded on an epidemiological catastrophe. The diseases brought by the Europeans devastated the indige-
nous peoples who had not had time to develop natural immunities. They
were replaced by Europeans, South and East Asians, and especially by
Africans. Today, the Caribbean is possibly on the edge of a second epidemiological catastrophe through the spread of AIDS, a problem already
severe in Haiti and Puerto Rico and rapidly expanding through all of the
islands (except Cuba, whose controls have remained tough, intrusive, and
effective).

Civil Society

Despite the best efforts of some of the first European conquerors and subsequent slave owners, the Caribbean has long featured a vibrant civil society marked especially by extensive voluntary and involuntary migration and the deep commitments of many to religious and philosophical communities of many kinds. In the 1990s, the Caribbean witnesses the wedding between some forms of migration and the spread of transnational criminality, as well as the exacerbation of religious interdenominational competition, nearly everywhere, but especially in Puerto Rico and Trinidad. The secular NGOs, moreover, recall to some degree the missionaries of old—committed, focused, resourceful, creative, generous, bearers of new wisdom, but also occasionally ignorant, arrogant, self-righteous, and pursuing agendas defined in the first instance from concerns derived outside of the region.

To the great dismay of European missionaries at mid-millennium and of governments ever since, informality has been a long-standing marker in Caribbean attitudes and behavior. Informality has applied to sex partnerships for centuries, where the census at times reports that the number of "free unions" exceeds that of formalized marriages. Informality is evident in religious practices, where Caribbean peoples have borrowed, invented, adapted, and preserved a joyful and complex variety of religious beliefs and practices. Informality is equally notable in linguistic practices, where Creole languages have been constructed on most islands to coexist with the languages imported from Europe.

Businesses that operate profitably and on a grand scale beyond the reach of government regulation, and nonstate actors armed with weapons and resources that challenge governments, have long been part of the Caribbean scene. They once were called smugglers and pirates, but they always have included many small businesses and individuals who consider themselves "good people," though they operate beyond the reach of the law. Informal economies and informal armies are part of this region's past and present. Today's most worrisome heirs of this informality are, of course, the violent drug traffickers.

Politics

Contrary to its reputation for chaotic politics, the Caribbean has featured lasting stable rulers. Rafael Leónidas Trujillo and Joaquín Balaguer in the Dominican Republic, François and Jean-Claude Duvalier in Haiti, Fidel Castro in Cuba, Eric Williams in Trinidad, Forbes Burnham in Guyana,

Eugenia Charles in Dominica, the Bird family in Antigua, and Luis Muñoz Marín in Puerto Rico are all extremely different from each other on many dimensions but one—they governed their countries for a very long time.

More impressively, the Anglophone Caribbean, along with Venezuela, Colombia, and Costa Rica represent the single set of countries, regionally defined, in the so-called Third World that have sustained democratic political systems for the longest period of time, witnessing repeated and peaceful turnovers of power from government to opposition. In more recent years, however, there is greater uncertainty about the future politics of Haiti, Cuba, Venezuela, and Colombia, and also about the evidence of growing criminal violence in several Caribbean and Central American countries, as well as in Colombia and Venezuela. In terms of political stability or democratic practices, there is the worry that the future may be worse than the past.

Governments in the Caribbean have always had high ambitions, though more limited capacities. The old forts—vast in Cartagena de Indias, more modest in St. Kitts—recall the efforts of many to make their lands invulnerable to international forces. The history of each records several instances when such mighty fortifications were overcome. The governments of the region have sought to shape their societies and their economies to varying degrees—Cuba the most among them—but they have been discovering in the 1990s that their limitations and incapacities may require them at last to curtail their statist preferences. Even "fortress Cuba," Fidel Castro has discovered to his great reluctance, has been compelled to recognize the limitations of its state's hoped-for omnipotence.

In response to intrusive international attempts to organize behavior in the Caribbean in the times of colonial empires or, later on, when supposedly independent governments in the region were allegedly not up to the job, many peoples in the Caribbean, and often many of the governments, have cooperated little with outsiders—not even with other governments in the region. The Caribbean can be defined irreverently as a set of islands with their backs to the sea, and to each other. Even some of the countries on the mainland—whether Guyana or Venezuela—could be described as islands surrounded by land, and equally marked for having turned their backs on their neighbors. Faced with relentless and persistent insularity, governments in the Anglophone Caribbean and more gradually those of other countries have been looking for forms of collaboration. The Anglophones began to cooperate in the 1950s. Cuba and Venezuela "discovered" the Caribbean politically in the 1970s, Colombia did so in the 1980s, and U. S. policy in the 1980s forced the Caribbean and Central American governments to acknowledge that others perceived them as part of the same "Basin." The Association of Caribbean States is the most recent and far-reaching of the efforts of governments of the region to act as though they were united by the sea that washes up on their shores.

Colonized for centuries, and the object of U. S. intervention in this century, the Caribbean remains the object of sustained international tutelage over the economic practices of its governments (the "tutors" are the international financial institutions, the major European governments, Canada, and the United States) and also the object of international pressures to foster or consolidate democracy, and especially for fair and free elections—pressures evident in the 1990s, especially in Cuba, the Dominican Republic, Guyana, Haiti, and Suriname. Outside powers contribute less to the Caribbean than in times past, but seem to demand no less.

In this book, we explore several dimensions of Caribbean security and insecurity in the broad context previously suggested. We focus special attention on the islands but also consider to some degree most of the other countries on the mainland that border on the Caribbean sea. We do so because the themes sketched earIler retain special importance today and in the years ahead.

James N. Rosenau's chapter views the Caribbean as a specific example of a much broader international pattern. He argues that the Caribbean can be viewed as an expression of a central tension that pervades world affairs, namely, the tension that derives from the simultaneity of pressures toward centralization, integration, and globalization on the one hand, and those pulling in decentralizing, fragmenting, and localizing directions on the other. These tensions, he avers, are powerful and continuous. He analyzes the components of these international and domestic collisions by examining the likelihood of cooperation and conflict as well as the prospects both for state-centric and multicentric social and political organization. He has coined the term *fragmegration* to label this mixture of processes at work in the Caribbean and, more generally, in the international system.

Anthony T. Bryan takes a different approach. He focuses directly on the Caribbean to discern the major challenges faced by the governments and peoples of the region. He explores the shift in the region's political economy, leading countries toward market openings, and also assesses the renewed strain on democratic governance in various countries (Trinidad and Tobago, Venezuela) where attempts have been made to overthrow governments by force and where such attempts have succeeded (Haiti). He notes, moreover, that the quality of democratic practice has weakened, as evidenced in declining voter turnouts, at the same moment that the overextended state is compelled to reduce many of its activities. He also calls attention to the Caribbean's premier international issues: migration, drug trafficking, the environment, the defense of democracy, and international trade integration.

Andrés Serbin links Rosenau's and Bryan's chapters by exploring first the global challenges that broad international trends pose for the region and second the process of regionalization within the Caribbean Basin that has been deepening interconnectedness among the countries of the region. In so doing, Serbin challenges older international relations approaches that are insufficiently sensitive to the multitiered reality of the Caribbean, long embedded in the international system, enveloped by global economic trends, but also rooted in the particularity of distinctive societies. Serbin explores in some detail various creative efforts to deepen and widen Caribbean regional integration, paying special attention to the Association of Caribbean States (ACS), established in July 1994. The ACS includes the islands (Cuba among them) and the countries of the mainland touched by the Caribbean Sea, except the United States. Serbin analyzes the attempt of the ACS to function as an entity in itself and also as a bridge connecting other integration schemes in the Americas to foster economic growth and consolidate democratic governance.

Jorge I. Domínguez focuses more narrowly on the Caribbean as an international political system to examine aspects of continuity and change. He argues that many aspects of the Caribbean's international experience have long-standing historical roots, among them the presence of superpower military hegemony, political and economic polycentricity, unauthorized international migration, and the powerful violence of nonstate military forces. The "units" in this international subsystem have never been just states. The Caribbean has also long been the object of attempts by major powers to impose international norms on the region, be it the abolition of the slave trade in the nineteenth century or the defense of markets in the late twentieth century. Domínguez argues, however, that the Caribbean is witnessing three major international structural changes: the military hegemony of one superpower is at last uncontested, quasistate military forces are no longer significant, and nonstate military forces have become more important than at any time since the Napoleonic Wars. He notes that the normative disposition to international intervention (military, political, economic) in the Caribbean also has risen markedly.

Ivelaw L. Griffith explores the geography of drug trafficking in the Caribbean. He locates the Caribbean as the spatial vortex of this traffic and demonstrates the ease of operation for international criminal syndicates. He identifies in some detail the patterns and methods of trafficking, providing in effect a census of these activities across the countries of the region. He explains the physical and social geography features that facilitate the movement of drugs from South American producer countries to consumer countries in North America. Geography is, however, not as vital an element in the trans-shipment links with Europe; although geography helps explain the Caribbean-South American part of the trafficking to Europe, political ties between Caribbean and European countries, and the resulting commercial and immigration arrangements, are the key factors in this case. Griffith also examines the creativity and ingenuity of the drug operators and the people who collude with them, as well as the complex social organization, which characterize the traffic. Griffith considers the region's narcotics operations a manifestation of some of the dangerous dynamics of the interconnections of drugs, geography, power, and politics in the region.

Richard J. Bloomfield discusses the prospects for collective security mechanisms in the Caribbean. He identifies three peculiarities of security threats in the Caribbean: they are rooted in domestic social and economic problems, initiated by nonstate actors, and elude the control of governments. He assesses the utility of existing collective security mechanisms to address the potential security threats in the Caribbean and concludes that the mechanisms are not especially pertinent for the problems the Caribbean faces. Bloomfield concentrates instead on the defense of democracy as the principal objective of collective security endeavors in the region and argues that subregional collective security arrangements may be more effective than other forms of organizations at reaching this goal. He notes persuasively that continued U. S. involvement in the affairs of Caribbean countries is "inevitable," thus the practical choice for Caribbean countries is how to harness and shape such involvement toward constructive ends.

This book ends with a broad assessment of regional security prepared by Venezuela's Institute for Advanced Study in National Defense, a think tank that informs the strategic analyses of Venezuela's armed forces. The Institute takes the view that drug trafficking, migration, the environment, and democratic stability, as well as rules and institutions for international collaboration, are part of the agenda for regional security. It affirms the value of democracy and the utility of international cooperation to advance and safeguard the shared goals of the peoples of the region.

The authors of this book do not agree on every topic, but the editors have chosen not to impose an artificial consensus. Instead, we hope readers will sharpen their own understanding of the issues by reading convergent but different analyses. The authors differ, for example, concerning the definition of the region. Bryan, Griffith, and Domínguez emphasize the islands as the core of their analysis, while Bloomfield, Serbin, and the Institute employ a geographically wider definition. Another difference is evident in the definition of security. Bloomfield and Domínguez rely on a strict definition of security (directly related to the use of force), whereas Serbin and the

Institute employ a more comprehensive notion of security that encompasses environmental threats and migration, among other issues.

We all agree, however, that the affairs of the Caribbean are best understood as deriving from the combination of the domestic and the international, conscious as well that governments alone have never been the only actors in the Caribbean's relations with the world. We affirm the proposition that the region's future depends on addressing concerns that go well beyond traditional definitions of security. And, as in the title of Rosenau's chapter, we are conscious of both the accidental, though recurrent, as well as the structural aspects of international intrusions on the affairs of the Caribbean and, we would also add, of the Caribbean's intrusion on the interests of the people and government of the United States.

2

HURRICANES ARE NOT THE ONLY INTRUDERS

The Caribbean in an Era of Global Turbulence

JAMES N. ROSENAU

The Caribbean reality at the end of the twentieth century is tantalizingly difficult to define. . . . The region is like a prism with light passing through—whatever enters is transformed. This leads to enormous imprecision in self-definition . . . and a veritable nightmare for statisticians, demographers, and especially those obsessed with color and race. Nothing in the Caribbean is simple. . . . Even the term "Caribbean" can be subject to various political and geographical definitions.[1]

Islands are different. The seas serve as a barrier and as a highway. Island peoples are intensely attached and loyal to their birthplace. Yet, as economic needs dictate, they easily move to other islands or to the mainland—but always intending to return to their homeland.[2]

Our vulnerability is manifold. Physically, we are subject to hurricanes and earthquakes; economically, to market decisions taken elsewhere, socially, to cultural penetration; and now politically, to the machinations of terrorists, mercenaries, and criminals.[3]

L ike every other region, these epigraphs are saying, in effect, that the Caribbean has unique characteristics, even as it is also subject to intrusive winds of change from abroad. Here limitations of space and training allow only for emphasis on the latter, on the global dynamics that may affect the capacity of Caribbean states to achieve collective security.

Perhaps there are some virtues to not being a specialist on the region. Viewing the world through the eyes of a generalist denies one the capacity to make specific policy recommendations or even to comment meaningfully about current situations; but at the same time, the generalist can bring to bear some propositions about the dynamics presently driving world politics that may have relevance for an understanding of Caribbean issues and their potential for both amelioration and intensification. In addition, and no less relevant, nonspecialists are not heavily ensconced in the history of the region, which is an advantage in the sense that they can look at its problems through fresh eyes and more freely recognize how the dynamics of change sweeping the world may render long-standing precedents and seemingly intractable memories less and less central to the course of events in the Caribbean. The nonspecialist is not encumbered (if that is the right word) by the need to engage in analyses that duly take note of the history of dictatorial regimes in Haiti, the decades-long dominance of the United States in the region, the recurrent controversies over the Panama Canal, the ups and downs of relations with Cuba, and those moments in the past marked by efforts to develop region-wide institutions designed to resolve conflicts and promote prosperity. Such enduring matters are surely relevant to present circumstances, but at the same time they can obscure the significance of relatively recent transformations at work on a global scale and how these may also have an impact on Caribbean affairs.

Such, then, is the purpose of this chapter. First, it seeks to contrast some of the major aspects of global politics undergoing deep change and those that remain relatively constant, and, second, an attempt is made to suggest ways in which these contrasts may be relevant to security considerations in the Caribbean. Throughout, it is assumed that the changes are sufficiently powerful to have altered the postures and capabilities of states, as well as to have broadened the range of actors who participate in the international arena. It is this assumption that frees the analysis from the need to highlight historical landmarks and facilitates treating the present era as a time when economic, social, and political dynamics may be altering institutions and framing new arrangements through which to conduct international, regional, national, and local affairs.

THREE CAVEATS

Before proceeding, however, some caveats are in order. Assessing the consequences of change runs the risk of exaggeration, of treating people and societies as so malleable that they shift their fundamental practices with ease and without resistance. So it is important to note at the outset that while major transformations are at work on the world scene, they are not so thoroughgoing as to overwhelm the habits and inertia to which individuals, groups, and governments have long been accustomed. We must perforce focus on discernible tendencies and not wholesale shifts, on incremental changes expressive of underlying patterns and not revolutionary changes reflective of reversals in direction. The Caribbean Basin is different today than it was only a few years ago, but the differences are not so great as to erase the grip that culture and habit have over its peoples. Put differently, while sensitivities to "regionness" have intensified around the world,[4] the focus here is on a particular region that is adapting to global changes through its own unique cultural lenses and historical circumstances.[5]

This is another way of emphasizing that while the ensuing analysis focuses on dynamics operative on a global scale, they are not posited as having the same impacts and consequences in all parts of the world. On the contrary, due to historical, cultural, economic, geographic, and a host of other factors, the transformations underway throughout the world are conceived to unfold unevenly in both pace and direction. The formulation developed later stresses that the transformations are evolving everywhere, but that is not to assume that they are doing so in a uniform fashion. The Caribbean is no more immune to any of the worldwide dynamics than any other region; at the same time, the way in which these dynamics play out in the archipelago can vary substantially from their impacts and consequences elsewhere in the world. Just as hurricanes have variable impacts, so do the winds of turbulence blow across world politics with differing velocities and in different directions.[6]

Next, it is important to acknowledge at the outset that our view of the problems and dynamics of the region are in good part the result of some basic theoretical premises we bring to bear on the subject. Whether we are generalists or area specialists, and irrespective of whether or not we are conscious of our underlying orientations, we cannot help but proceed on the basis of conceptual understandings of what motivates individuals, what sustains their collectivities, and what shapes the interactions among them. There are no object realities inherent in the Caribbean Basin around which all observers can converge. One analyst's "truth" is another's irrelevancy. Why? Because the whole story of the Caribbean can never be told. It consists of too much detail to be grasped in its entirety. Perforce, therefore, we have to select some phenomena as important and dismiss others as trivial, an intellectual process that can lead to wide intersubjective consensuses but cannot pretend to portray objective circumstances. To be sure, for example, the region is comprised mostly of islands; and yes, such geographic configurations can be consequential in a number of ways; but how their significance gets interpreted is not self-evident. The relevance of archipelago variables depends on how much causal potency we attach to geographic factors, and the attribution of potency in turn depends on the theoretical baggage we bring to bear. And so it is with respect to our presumptions about the relative strength of historical continuities and breakpoints, states and citizens, economics and politics, and any other aspects of the region that may command our analytic attention. Put differently, it matters whether we are essentially realists who deny the dynamics of change and approach the Caribbean as a site where the only meaningful actions are initiated by states ever ready to be conflictual, or whether our perceptual range also allows for transformations that lead states to pursue cooperative goals and opens up the political arena to a wide range of other types of actors in the region who contribute significantly to the conduct of its affairs.[7]

In short, any order we claim to be operative in the Caribbean is an order we impose upon it. The need to maintain a measure of brevity in our descriptions may lead us to refer to the underlying order of Caribbean affairs, but it is nonetheless an analytically imposed order, a set of arrangements that we view as recurrent, precisely because we regard them as inherent in the actors and practices we treat as salient.

This is not to say, of course, that there are no criteria by which the utility of a theoretical perspective can be assessed. To presume our understanding is deeply conditioned by our theories is not to give license to any and all observations that may strike our fancy. Concepts must be clearly specified and some basic rules of evidence must be followed, even though objective realities lie beyond our grasp. A fundamental discipline, in other words, must underlie our work if our insights and findings are to contribute to a widely shared intersubjective consensus regarding current conditions and future potentials in the Caribbean region.

Last, given a world that is undergoing profound transformations, we need to keep in mind that we are focusing on complex processes in which cause and effect often occur almost simultaneously and are thus so interactive as to render conventional social science practices unusable. To treat certain phenomena as independent variables and others as dependent variables is not a methodology that lends itself to tracing the global dynamics considered relevant here. Because these dynamics are so pervasive and powerful, what is an outcome of change at one moment in time can be a stimulus to further change in the very next moment, thereby confounding any effort to sort out first-order from second-order causes and effects. This problem could be handled by freezing action in time and place—by separating one moment from the next so the links between causes and effects can be readily observed—but to do so would be to assume the profundity of the dynamics that are transforming the conduct of global affairs.

THE TURBULENCE MODEL AND FIVE IMPOSED ORDERS

There is no lack of explanation for the transformation reconfiguring world politics today. The most widely cited concerns the end of the cold war and the resulting release of energies, aspirations, and challenges that had long been stifled by the superpower competition. While there can be little doubt that the momentous developments of 1989–1991 had enormous consequences for every community and country in the world, to posit the end of the cold war as a source of current situations is not to explain why these are unfolding as they are. It only points to the removal of prior conditions and does not highlight the underlying conditions that presently sustain the energies, aspirations, and challenges that are altering institutions and shaping the course of events. Accordingly, the focus here is on the transformative dynamics that continue to be operative, perhaps somewhat less conspicuously than when they contributed to an end to the cold war but nonetheless still very much a source of the changes and continuities that mark the world scene.

As elaborated upon at great length elsewhere,[8] three basic parameters of the global system can usefully be treated as undergoing transformation on a global scale. One involves citizens at the micro level who are regarded as everywhere experiencing a skill revolution that has enabled them to perceive more clearly where they fit in the course of events and thus to engage more effectively in collective actions designed to serve their interests. A second transformation is seen as occurring at what can be called the macro-micro level, through which individuals are linked to their collectivities: the argument here is that collectivities everywhere, governments and nongovernmental organizations alike, are undergoing authority crises in which traditional conceptions of legitimacy are being replaced by performance criteria of legitimacy, thus fostering organizational disarray, stalemate, restructuring, and proliferation, that in turn enhances the readiness of individuals to employ their newly acquired skills on behalf of their perceived self-interests. A third transformation is considered to be unfolding at the macro level of global structure; here, processes of bifurcation are viewed as giving rise to two worlds of world politics—a state-centric world composed of national governments and sovereign states, and a multicentric world comprised of diverse nongovernmental actors who are independent of the state-centric world and who frequently conflict, cooperate, or otherwise interact with counterparts in the state-centric world—that are still working out their respective domains as the foundations of the emergent global order.

These three parametric transformations are conceived as having been underway well before the end of the Cold War. Indeed, the turbulence model posits their inception as having occurred some four decades ago and as likely to continue for the foreseeable future. They are also seen as both sources and consequences of two other dynamics that are not so much parameters of the system as they are basic processes that fuel and are fueled by each of the parametric transformations. I have in mind here the processes of globalization and localization and the links between them, what some refer to as "glocalization" and what I have elsewhere called the processes of "fragmegration" on the grounds that this term nicely captures the simultaneity and interaction of those forces propelling collectivities toward integration and those spurring fragmentation. Viewed as a single dynamic, the processes of fragmegration are posited as tapping into the skill revolution by sensitizing people to the possibility that the identity and basis of their citizenship may be changing, as tapping into many authority crises by redirecting loyalties and legitimacy sentiments, which in turn are altering the allegiances collectivities can command, and as tapping into the bifurcation of global structures by weakening the sovereignty and competence of states and hastening the formation or consolidation of collectivities in the multicentric world.

Stated differently, any extant situations today, including those that comprise Caribbean affairs, can be viewed as expressions of a central tension that pervades world affairs, namely the tension that derives from the simultaneity of pressures toward centralization, integration, and globalization on the one hand, and those pulling in decentralizing, fragmenting, and localizing directions on the other. This tension may not always have the force of hurricane winds, but it is powerful and continuous and it is propelling individuals, groups, communities, countries, and international regions into new forms of economic, social, and political organization.

Having devoted an entire book and a number of subsequent essays to spelling out this conception of the underlying dynamics driving world politics,[9] it is tempting to elaborate and seek to demonstrate the accuracy of the conception. In the interest of addressing how the turbulence model and the dynamics of fragmegration may be applicable to Caribbean affairs, however, I shall resist this temptation and simply ask the reader to play my game and temporarily assume that this formulation offers an accurate assessment of the paths that are leading the world into the future.

Yet, before an application can be undertaken, we need to address the aforementioned problem wherein our understanding of Caribbean affairs is in good part a consequence of the order we impose upon them. That is, if one is inclined to rely on a synthesis of the turbulence and fragmegration models, where might such an approach fit in relation to other possible ways of imposing order on the region? My response is to focus on the various orders analysts and practitioners impose on global politics as a consequence of their presumptions regarding the identity of the central actors on the world stage and the direction of their actions. By distinguishing between actors that are states and those that are not, and by differentiating those actors that view the world as essentially conflictual from those that regard it as essentially cooperative, it becomes possible to identify the primary forms of order to which most analysts subscribe. There are five such forms, and the logic of their derivation and juxtaposition can be seen in Figure 2.1.[10]

Four of these forms are familiar, although the labels attached to them may differ from those used here. Perhaps the most familiar is the *unilateral* order (often called realism) in which analysts and practitioners conceive of the course of events as driven by states and their governments. All other actors are seen as essentially peripheral and subject to the will of states. There is no higher authority to which states must respond and through which international order and justice is maintained. States have to preserve their independence and well-being through self-help and the maximization of their power relevant to other states. They may cooperate with other states through alliances and intergovernmental organizations (IGOs) if it is in their immediate interest, but they are seen as being ready at all times to break any commitments they have made to more encompassing international systems if unilateral and conflictual actions are seen as better enabling them to realize their subsystemic goals in a distrustful and hostile world. To impose a unilateral order on events, in short, is to perceive the world as an anarchic system that fosters conflict in the absence of enduring authorities with which states must comply.[11]

Other observers and practitioners impose a second form of order in which it is assumed that in this era of ever-expanding complexity the predominance of states is unchallenged, but that their interdependence renders them sensitive to shared normative restraints and mindful of long-term goals, which can incline them to engage in multilateral cooperation despite their immediate interests. Thus, states are seen as willing to accord

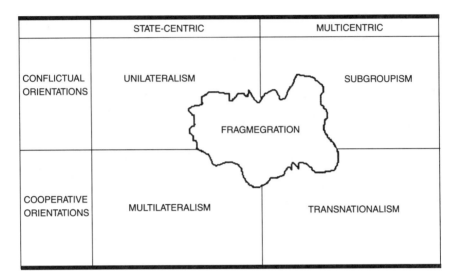

FIGURE 2.1 Five Imposed Orders

a measure of autonomy and authority to the institutions and regimes of the global system with respect to certain issues, even as they may unilaterally pursue their subsystemic concerns on other questions. In this perceived *multilateral* order (often referred to as a liberal order) the world is not so much anarchic as it is a system of balanced constraints that allow for cooperation and inhibit states from clinging to narrow self-interests.[12]

Still other observers and practitioners, impressed by the erosion of the authority of states and the clamor of long-standing ethnic minorities for recognition, have come to perceive the basic structures of world politics as having undergone a bifurcation in which the state-centric world must now interact with a multicentric world composed of subnational, national, and transnational collectivities that have extended the key structures well beyond the interstate system. Both as sources and consequences of the bifurcation, the forces of fragmentation are seen as proliferating, the centers of authority as fraying, and the world stage as so dense with actors that all of them have little choice but to enhance their own narrow self-interests. Like states, in other words, numerous actors in many segments of the multicentric world are presumed to distrust cooperative arrangements and be inclined toward narrow, self-serving courses of action. In effect, they place their subsystemic interests well ahead of larger systemic needs and aspirations. In so doing, they seek out like-minded others in their close-at-

hand environment for support and psychic comfort, a process that is perhaps best designated as "subgroupism." This term is conceived to be more
generic than that of "nationalism," since there are many other groups besides nations that have cohered more fully around common identities and
sought thereby to advance shared goals. It is not mere coincidence, for example, that in addition to secessionist movements in Europe and Russia,[13]
such diverse collectivities as the Mafia, youth gangs, the Palestinians, the
Zapatistas, and the residents of Staten Island, have simultaneously
experienced rampant subgroupism. Nor does the relocation of authority
inherent in this powerful tendency toward subsystems and away from
whole systems necessarily reach an end point. It is the nature of the
process that subgroupism begets subgroupism (as Quebec presses for
autonomy from Canada, for example, so do the Mohawks press for autonomy within Quebec), with the result that tendencies toward conflict tend
to sustain the dynamics of subgroupism. Accordingly, taken together with
states, the bifurcated global system is regarded as closely resembling the
decentralized structures of the medieval era. When analysts and practitioners impose this neomedieval form of pluralist order[14]—or what I pre-
fer to call a *subgroupist* order—the world is seen as highly decentralized,
conflictual, and disorderly.[15]

A fourth group of analysts and practitioners share the premise that
greater interdependence has eroded the authority of states, intensified the
relevance and salience of other types of actors and thus brought into being
bifurcated structures; but they also perceive these tendencies as having
heightened the necessity of cooperation and as rendering less salient those
that foster conflict. This imposed order posits the world stage less as populated with subnational collectivities and more as crowded with NGOs,
transnational corporations, social movements, professional societies, epis-
temic communities, and other private entities concerned with environmental, humanitarian, and developmental goals that incline them toward
participation in international regimes and organizations in search of cooperative solutions. In imposing this *transnational* form of order, analysts and
practitioners conceive of the global system as being increasingly founded
on a multiplicity of institutionalized and ad hoc arrangements through
which governments and nongovernmental collectivities accommodate
each other and, in so doing, come to share responsibility for the course of
events in a crazy-quilt and yet systemic fashion.[16]

The fifth form of imposed order is less widely shared and unfamiliar
to many analysts. It also is the paradigm that I employ to explain the course
of events. As indicated by the space in the middle of Figure 2.1, my way of
imposing order is to proceed from the presumption that the real order

encompasses the pervasive contradictions in world affairs, powerful tendencies toward systemic cooperation and subsystemic conflict are both likely to endure, thus, all four of the other imposed orders reflect some part of the true state of affairs. As I see it, the bifurcation of the global system allows for, in effect, unilateralism, multilateralism, subgroupism, and transnationalism all to be operative in global life, sometimes reinforcing each other and sometimes negating each other but at all times at work in one part of the world or another. As a result, the underlying order is viewed as sustaining deep-seated processes that foster both conflict and cooperation.

The terminology available to characterize and analyze this complex order is insufficient. The present offers no dominant relationship such as the superpower competition that underlay the labeling of the Cold War. Nor is the present distribution of power so self-evident as to warrant recourse to hegemonic or balance-of-power labels. Some have suggested that it be designated a polyarchical order because of the absence of an unmistakable and simple hierarchy among states,[17] but this seems unsuitable in that it implies the new global order rests on a static set of structural arrangements and fails to indicate the tensions between the fragmenting consequences of conflict and the integrative effects of cooperation. Perhaps even less suitable is a terminology that characterizes the present period as "the post-Cold War order." Such a label is "tentative, vague; it lacks authority";[19] and it is insufficient as well because even as it concedes the presence of patterns yet to form, it also may mislead us into overlooking or downplaying the emergence of processes that systematically link globalizing and localizing dynamics.

What is needed, in short, is a terminology that suggests neither a relationship nor a pecking order; rather, a label is needed that calls attention to the basic processes on which the emergent order is based. So it is that I fall back on the contrived and synthesized designation noted earlier—fragmegration. While the label may seem awkward at first, it nonetheless points out the simultaneous and interactive links between the dynamics fragmenting some collectivities and integrating others. Given the contradictions and complexity of a fragmegrative order, the world is seen as short on clear-cut distinctions between domestic and foreign affairs, with the result that local problems can become transnational in scope even as global challenges can have repercussions for small communities. In effect, in the fragmegrated order, the global system is so disaggregated that it lacks overall patterns and, instead, is marked by various structures of systemic cooperation and subsystemic conflict in different regions, countries, and issue areas. This variability is extensive enough to justify labeling the overall order as one of *uneven fragmegration,* a term that is highlighted by the ragged edges of the space in the center of Figure 2.1 and that further captures the diversity of the underlying order.[19]

UNILATERALISM AND THE CARIBBEAN

While unilateralists may not deny that basic parameters of the global system have undergone transformation or that processes of globalization are underway everywhere, neither do they attach any relevance to such changes insofar as the Caribbean is concerned. Imposing a unilateralist order on the region has long been the conventional way of understanding the central dynamics of Caribbean affairs, and unilateralists discern no good basis for altering this convention. Whether analysts are Americans or citizens of one of the Caribbean countries, they stress that states are the dominant actor and that the region is inherently conflictual because one of the states, the United States, is so much more powerful than the others and has never had difficulty finding reasons to intervene in Caribbean affairs, when its interests seem threatened. Never mind that things have changed, a unilateralist would argue; the fact remains that the United States so fully commands the hemispheric scene that the potential of American intervention is so great and obvious as to be the central reality of the region. From the perspective of unilateralism, an excerpt from a 1927 State Department memorandum by Undersecretary of State Robert Olds still captures this quintessential truth:

> Our ministers accredited to the five little republics stretching from the Mexican border to Panama . . . have been advisers whose advice has been accepted virtually as law in the capitals where they respectively reside. . . . We do control the destinies of Central America and we do so for the simple reason that the national interest absolutely dictates such a course. . . . Until now Central America has always understood that governments which we recognize and support stay in power, while those we do not recognize and support fail.[20]

Such wording may seem brazen today, unilateralists would concede, but it is nonetheless a bedrock perspective, no matter how delicately it may be put.

Nor is this simply a U. S. orientation. A unilateralist approach stresses the large extent to which a complimentary orientation can readily be found in the attitudes of Caribbean officials, who cannot help but be aware of the disparities of power and the American readiness to resort to military force if it deems that a situation is getting out of hand. To be sure, lately it has exercised its power on behalf of decent democratic values, as in its 1994 invasion that toppled a military regime and restored a duly elected president in Haiti; but however high-minded such actions may be, they still represent the imposition of U. S. will on the region. Furthermore, from a unilateralist perspective, it is the orientation of the United States that makes the difference, both when the countries of the hemisphere act collectively and when they have difficulty doing so. As one analyst put it in the context of all Latin American countries, "To come together successfully requires that they either flatly oppose the U. S. or cooperate with it."[21]

Unilateralism leads to a similar conclusion when the potential for collective action in the region rather than the potential for U. S. intervention serves as the question to be addressed. Ever ready to perceive states as conflictual, the unilateralist stresses that the mechanisms for collective action developed by the countries of the region are insufficient to be effective, that the various states continue to cling to their own particular interests, thus are reluctant to give highest priority to regional interests. Accordingly, despite acknowledging that both internal attitudes and external contexts are changing, a number of specialists concluded "the will to take collective action has not taken root in all of Latin America."[22]

MULTILATERALISM AND THE CARIBBEAN

A very different picture of the region emerges from the imposition of a multilateralist perspective that posits states as continuing to be the dominant actors but also sees them as having moved from conflictual to cooperative orientations. Whether the shift to cooperative impulses derives from states being more responsive to skilled publics who are more capable of challenging their authority is not of concern to multilateralists. They simply assume the shift has occurred and highlight its breadth by pointing to extensive networks of IGOs in which the various Caribbean states have become involved. In addition, the shift is conceived as a metaphoric hurricane intruding upon the region from diverse directions. One storm center is the United States, which is perceived to have ameliorated the force of its winds through a major policy transformation in "the direction of regarding the hemisphere more as a partnership,"[23] with its adherence to NAFTA reflecting a new "emphasis upon parity . . . in the U. S. attitude toward its neighbors."[24] No less powerful as a force for change are the worldwide tendencies among states to seek resolutions of long-standing issues—what might be called the "globalization of cooperation"[25]—tendencies that are readily evident in the United Nations' (UN's) greater readiness to cross the divide between domestic and foreign affairs and become involved in the internal life of its members when elections are contested, civil wars turn genocidal, human rights are grossly violated, development needs are acute, the natural environment is threatened, and so on, through all of the situations that comprise the global agenda. Perhaps even more important, the globalization of cooperation is also viewed as spreading to local, subregional, and regional levels: in the words of two longtime observers, "Whatever the United Nations purports to be doing at the global level today in the realm of social and economic development, more effective action is taking place at [a] regional level—in East Asia, South Asia, Latin America, and Africa—where regional organizations are increasingly active and respected."[26] In short, for a variety of reasons linked to the world's ever-growing interdependence, "There does appear to be a new attitude in the hemisphere and in the world that the international community does have common interests and should pursue these interests collectively."[27]

Multilateralists also discern both positive and negative incentives toward cooperation in the specific circumstances of Caribbean states. On the positive side is "a growing confidence that they can play a much larger role in solving their problems through their own actions."[28] On the other hand, some part of a reinvigorated cooperative impulse stems from negative incentives and the need to cope cooperatively with the emergence of a global economy that poses threats from a variety of diverse directions:

> At their root is the question of the role the region might play in the world economic order of the 1990s and beyond. Several trends that pose a danger to existing economic practices can be identified: the globalization of markets for goods, services, capital, and technology, which imperils the region's wage cost and location advantages in relation to North American investment; the general dematerialization of industrial production, which bodes ill for commodity producers; the strengthening of economic blocs in North America [via NAFTA] and Western Europe [via EU], which threatens access to traditional markets for "uncompetitive" agricultural export staples, manufactured goods, and services; the emergence of the Pacific Rim as a pole of growth, which cannot but marginalize the Caribbean as a source of dynamic business opportunities; the transformation of Eastern Europe into a market economy, which seems likely to divert trade and aid in its direction; and the failure of the international community collectively to deal with the problem of Third World debt, which threatens Caribbean states, as others, with a continuation of debilitating service payments and consequent diminished growth.[29]

Little wonder, then, that a leading politician of the region, the prime minister of Trinidad and Tobago, has often been cited for his warning in 1989 that the Caribbean was in danger of "becoming a backwater, separated from the main current of human advance into the twenty-first century."[30]

In addition, the global transformations contribute to cooperative incentives by altering and, in important ways, expanding the conditions under which interventions into the region from abroad might occur. While the threat of U. S. interventions has diminished with the end of cold war competition, today "the issues that might lead to some form of international intervention, such as environmental degradation, drug trafficking, human rights abuses, and the state of democracy are the kind that are of concern to large parts of the international community. No longer can it be assumed that intervention will be presented in the guise of David vs. Goliath; rather, it may be the good guys vs. the bad guys, with those resisting outside pressures wearing the black hats."[31]

Much as analysts and practitioners discern a multiplicity of reasons why multilateral initiatives are likely to be undertaken and sustained in the Caribbean, however, they are not inclined to minimize the obstacles to greater region-wide cooperation.[32] The literature is pervaded with extensive awareness of the pitfalls that confront the Organization of American States (OAS), the Caribbean Community (CARICOM), and other IGOs intent upon increasing the coherence and collaboration of the various states. Some analysts enumerate a long list of reasons why the OAS still has a long way to go before it becomes an effective collective security mechanism. Others note the inherent contradiction between long-standing antipathies to external intervention and maintaining the region-wide momentum toward democratic regimes that has gathered strength in recent years. External interventions are viewed as noxious, but so are authoritarian regimes, all of which poses a dilemma because of emergent norms that allow for interventions that restore democratic institutions. On balance, however, a multilateral perspective posits cooperation within the region as an imperative—"We have to work together if we are to ensure that the Caribbean remains a zone of peace, prosperity, and democracy"[33]—and treats contrary tendencies as no more than impediments to an underlying and desirable momentum. One need only read *Time for Action*, the 1992 report of the West Indian Commission, to sense the considerable optimism that "the common identity which distinguishes the Caribbean people" will lead to ever-greater benefits from a growing cooperation among their states.

A measure of the underlying momentum toward multilateral cooperation can even be found in the complex question of how the region should be defined. While it is commonplace to set forth the pros and cons of one or another definition,[34] it seems clear that a definitional consensus does exist, but that it has not been constant. Rather, it has been a moving consensus, a movement that is expressive of the integrative side of fragmegrative dynamics. That is, the prevailing conception of what constitutes the Caribbean has moved increasingly in a more encompassing direction—from the English-speaking Caribbean to the archipelago to the Caribbean Basin (thus including the Central American states) to the littoral states (thus including Venezuela, Colombia, and Mexico). For the purposes of this chapter, any of these definitions are appropriate, since the distinctions among the various groupings are not nearly as important as the characteristics and circumstances they share. As one observer puts it, it is reasonable to assume

> that the sum of the experiences and understandings of the Caribbean outweigh the territorial differences or peculiarities. . . . [T]he region comprises one culture area in which common factors have forged a more-or-less common way of looking at life, the world, and their place in the scheme of things. . . . Moreover, the Caribbean peoples, with their distinctive artificial societies, common history, and common problems, seem to have more in common than the Texan and the New Yorker, or the Mayan Indian and the cosmopolite of Mexico City.[35]

SUBGROUPISM AND THE CARIBBEAN

While not denying the central role governments play as sources of conflict in Caribbean affairs, more than a few analysts do not confine their perspectives on conflict to the state-centric world. Rather, by positing the bifurcation of the global system, their analytic antennae include various nongovernmental entities in the multicentric world that intrude discord into the region. Historically, these have included European political parties, U. S. business firms, and the Catholic Church, all of whose activities and ideologies underlie a description of the region as "a major battleground where . . . numerous forces are vying for influence and power,"[26] but in recent years the prime focus of those who impose a subgroupist order has been on the drug trade and corruption, money laundering, and crime that has accompanied the surge of drug consumption and transshipment into virtually all of the region's countries. Indeed, the threat of these dynamics is seen as so serious that, because of "the openness and vulnerability of Caribbean societies," not to mention their geographic configurations, it is estimated that "drug barons can easily subvert their sovereignty and governability."[37] Put differently, so powerful is the drug trade in the region, and so enormous are the difficulties Caribbean states face in controlling its expansion, that it is likely to be increasingly hard for those who impose a unilateralist order to resist acknowledging the processes of bifurcation that have enabled the drug trade to become deeply ensconced in the region.

TRANSNATIONALISM AND THE CARIBBEAN

Although hardly oblivious of the problems and conflicts that the drug trade and international crime syndicates are inducing in the region, other analysts impose a transnational order on the Caribbean by focusing upon the ways in which global interdependence has fostered cooperative endeavors among nongovernmental groups in the region and between them and counterparts elsewhere in the world. Such a perspective stresses the emergence of global norms that advance human rights, free trade, and democratization, that in turn have led to a vast proliferation of transnational organizations on every continent and in every country. The countries of the Caribbean are all seen to be caught up in the networks formed by these transnational processes. Within the region, for example, no less than 211 not-for-profit NGOs have been identified as actively establishing or maintaining links among groups that span intraregional boundaries,[38] and this listing does not include the ties that political parties and multinational corporations fashion with supporters abroad. As one source put it,

> But something else has changed, or at least has matured. The West Indian people have not waited on Governments; they have integrated—in their own informal but highly effective way. Indeed, through culture and sport and non-governmental activity of every kind, they have been steadily building structures of unity of their own. They are more than ready to occupy formal structures of unity that the political establishment builds.[39]

UNEVEN FRAGMEGRATION AND THE CARIBBEAN

As previously noted, there is some measure of accuracy in all of the foregoing perspectives on the region. If allowance is made for variability across time and among the several countries of the Caribbean, the unilateral, multilateral, subgroupist, and transnational paradigms all serve as useful pieces with which to address the puzzles posed by the region. The unilateralist perspective is useful at those historical moments when the United

States is pressing its interests on one or another Caribbean state and thereby sensitizing all of them to their vulnerabilities to U. S. power. The multilateral perspective begins to account for the responsiveness of states in the region to cooperative initiatives designed to cope with new interdependence types of issues—such as the drug trade, environmental pollution, and currency crises—that no state can effectively address on its own. The subgroupist orientation provides a way of grasping how and why restless publics and corrupt officials turn to the drug trade and crime to alleviate their problems, thereby fostering authority crises that continually confront Caribbean governments and undermine the integrity of the borders they are supposed to protect. The transnational paradigm serves well the need to explain the ever-widening involvement of nongovernmental groups and organizations in the multicentric world beyond the Caribbean.

None of these perspectives, however, are particularly suited to explaining the multiple challenges to the security of the region and the ways in which they might collectively be met. It is here, in the complex arena where security needs are shaped by both domestic and foreign dynamics, that a fragmegrative approach can be especially fruitful. It highlights a number of dynamics that are not otherwise the subject of intense analysis—it clarifies how traditional conceptions of national sovereignty are insufficient to cope with the continuous flow of messages, money, disease, drugs, ideas, and people from abroad; it calls attention to the ways in which such globalizing forces are rendering the Caribbean ever more subject to complex external events and trends that, in turn, foster internal economic fluctuations, unemployment, restlessness, and drug consumption; it enables analysts to focus on the processes through which localizing, island-specific loyalties inhibit the capacity of the region to develop effective institutions designed to increase its collective security; it opens up analytic room for tracing the ways in which NGOs and other actors in the multicentric world are acting independently of governments to both preserve domestic preferences and absorb human rights, environmental, and other norms that are evolving abroad; and no less important, a fragmegrative perspective accords meaning to developments at the citizen level, where expanded analytic skills are likely to have important consequences for both democracy in the region and the ability of governments to conduct sensible foreign policies.[40]

In short, and to recur one more time to the hurricane metaphor, this approach enables observers to trace the swirling collisions generated by the clash of winds from offshore and those that are propelled from within the region. That is, equipped with the concept of fragmegration, analysts are more likely to concentrate on the interaction effects of contradictions and tensions at work in the region, and their policy recommendations are thus likely to stress how the many imperatives that call for the building of collective, region-wide institutions can only be met if account is also taken of the numerous impulses to serve island-centered needs. From a frag-megrative perspective, in other words, not only will the various states and NGOs of the region have to subordinate their particular interests and build region-wide mechanisms of cooperation, they will also have to ameliorate the domestic problems that derive from high unemployment, extensive poverty, drug consumption, and the many other reasons why people at all levels are "highly disposed to consume drugs which relax tensions, suppress worries and problems, manage stress in their lives, and give them a feeling of overcoming their problems and being on top of the world."[41] As one wise analyst put it years ago, "The problems are qualitative as well as quantitative—how communities are to be organized; the nature of national identities that are to be forged; the substantive meanings of varied styles of integrating individuals and groups into national and local and supranational communities; the mix of ideologies that can explain and rationalize and stabilize the processes of change."[42]

NOTES

I am grateful to Hongying Wang for her critical reactions to an earlier draft of "Hurricanes Are Not the Only Intruders: The Caribbean in an Era of Global Turbulence."

1. Franklin W. Knight, *The Caribbean: The Genesis of a Fragmented Nationalism* (New York: Oxford University Press, 1990, 2d ed.), 308–9.

2. Jan Rogozinski, *A Brief History of the Caribbean: From the Arawak and the Carib to the Present* (New York: Penguin Books, 1994), vii.

3. Address by L. Erskine Sandiford, prime minister of Barbados to 1990 CARICOM Summit, quoted in Ivelaw Lloyd Griffith, *The Quest for Security in the Caribbean: Problems and Promises in Subordinate States* (Armonk, N.Y.: M. E. Sharpe, 1993), 42.

4. See, for example, Bjorn Hettne, "The New Regionalism: Implications for Development and Peace," in Bjorn Hettne and Andras Inotai (eds.), *The New Regionalism: Implications for Global Development and International Security* (Helsinki: UNU World Institute for Development Economics Research, 1994), 1–49.

5. Andras Inotai, "The New Regionalism and Latin America," in Hettne and Inotai (eds.), *The New Regionalism*, 51–92.

6. It is worth noting that the analogy to hurricanes is not entirely metaphoric. Although I am not aware of such a link in the Caribbean, on

occasion the strong forces of nature become powerful political issues. Recent earthquakes in Mexico and Japan are illustrative in this regard. Indeed, the 1985 quake in Mexico precipitated a continuing "social temblor that affected everything. It legitimated the form of popular mobilization in Mexico" (Anthony DePalma, "The Quake That Shook Mexico Is Recalled," *New York Times*, September 19, 1995, A3).

7. For a lengthy discussion of how our underlying theories shape our conclusions about international affairs, see James N. Rosenau and Mary Durfee, *Thinking Theory Thoroughly: Coherent Approaches to an Incoherent World* (Boulder: Westview Press, 1995).

8. James N. Rosenau, *Turbulence in World Politics: A Theory of Change and Continuity* (Princeton: Princeton University Press, 1990).

9. The book is *Turbulence in World Politics*, and the essays have since been brought together in *Along the Domestic-Foreign Frontier*.

10. Both Figure 2.1 and the discussion about it are drawn from two sources: James N. Rosenau, "Multilateral Governance and the Nation-State System: A Post-Cold War Assessment," Occasional Paper #1 in Western Hemisphere Governance, Inter-American Dialogue (Washington, D. C. September 1995), 6–9, and Rosenau, *Along the Domestic-Foreign Frontier*, 47–51.

11. For succinct statements of the unilateral form of imposed order, see Robert H. Jackson and Alan James (eds.), *States in a Changing World: A Contemporary Analysis* (Oxford: Clarendon Press, 1993) and John J. Mearsheimer, "The False Promise of International Institutions," *International Security*, vol. 19 (winter 1994/95), 5–49.

12. Compelling illustrations of the multilateral form of imposed order can be found in Emanuel Adler and Beverly Crawford (eds.), *Progress in Postwar International Relations* (New York: Columbia University Press, 1991); James L. Richardson, "Asia-Pacific: The Case for Geopolitical Optimism," *The National Interest*, no. 38 (winter 1994/95), 28–39; Volker Rittberger (ed.), *Regime Theory and International Relations* (Oxford: Clarendon Press, 1993); and John Gerard Ruggie (ed.), *Multilateralism Matters: The Theory and Praxis of an Institutional Form* (New York: Columbia University Press, 1993). For a cogent articulation of the multilateral form of imposed order in which it is argued that the long-term history of international organizations has been more successful in facilitating progress and stability than is appreciated, see Craig Murphy, *International Organization and Industrial Change: Global Governance since 1850* (New York: Oxford University Press, 1994).

13. For a cogent account of these movements, see Alexis Heraclides, "Secessionist Conflagration: What Is to Be Done?" *Security Dialogue*, vol. 25 (September 1994), 283–94.

14. The possibility of a neomedieval order is set forth in Hedley Bull, *The Anarchical Society: The Study of Order in World Politics* (New York: Columbia University Press, 1977), 254–5.

15. A disquieting example of subgroupism as an underlying global order is available in Robert D. Kaplan, "The Coming Anarchy: How Scarcity, Crime, Overpopulation, Tribalism, and Disease Are Destroying the Social Fabric of Our Planet," *The Atlantic Monthly* (February 1994), 44–76.

16. For affirmations of the transnational form of order, see Kenichi Ohmae, *The Borderless World: Power and Strategy in the Interlinked Economy* (New York: HarperBusiness, 1990); Kenichi Ohmae, *The End of the Nation State: The Rise of Regional Economies* (New York: Free Press, 1995); and Thomas Risse-Kappen (ed.), *Bringing Transnational Relations Back In* (Cambridge: Cambridge University Press, 1995).

17. See, for example, Seyom Brown, *New Forces, Old Forces, and the Future of World Politics* (Glenview, Ill.: Scott Foresman and Co., 1988), chaps. 12 and 13.

18. Atlas, "Name That Era," 1.

19. The notion of uneven fragmegration was suggested by Michael Zurn's formulation of "uneven denationalization." See his "Globalization and Individualization as Challenges for World Politics," a paper presented at the 34th Annual Meeting of the International Studies Association (Acapulco: March 1993).

20. Quoted in Richard Millett, "Central American Paralysis," *Foreign Policy*, no. 39 (summer 1980), 101.

21. Peter Hakim, "Comment," in Carl Kaysen, Robert A. Pastor, and Laura W. Reed (eds.), *Collective Responses to Regional Problems: The Case of Latin America and the Caribbean* (Cambridge, Mass.: American Academy of Arts and Sciences, 1994), 142.

22. The conclusions drawn from an extensive discussion of this question are summarized in Brett Ashley Leeds and Carl Kaysen, "Rapporteur's Report," in Kaysen, Pastor, and Reed (eds.), *Collective Responses to Regional Problems*, 144.

23. Joe Clark, "Comment," in Kaysen, Pastor, and Reed (eds.), *Collective Responses to Regional Problems*, 126.

24. Joe Clark, "Comment," in Kaysen, Pastor, and Reed (eds.), *Collective Responses to Regional Problems*, 127.

25. For some empirical data that depict the globalization of cooperation as partly the result of a contagion effect, see James N. Rosenau, "Interdependence and the Simultaneity Puzzle: Notes on the Outbreak of Peace," in C.W. Kegley Jr. (ed.), *The Long Postwar Peace: Contending Explanations and Projections* (New York: Harper Collins Publishers, 1991), 307–28.

26. Roger A. Coate and Donald J. Puchala, "Global Policies and the United Nations System: A Current Assessment," *Journal of Peace Research,* vol. 27, no. 2 (1990), 139.

27. Leeds and Kaysen, "Rapporteur's Report," in Kaysen, Pastor, and Reed (eds.), *Collective Responses to Regional Problems,* 156.

28. Joe Clark, "Comment," in Kaysen, Pastor, and Reed (eds.), *Collective Responses to Regional Problems,* 126. For an earlier assertion along these lines, see David Lowenthal (ed.), *The West Indies Federation: Perspectives on a New Nation* (New York: Columbia University Press, 1961).

29. Anthony Payne and Paul Sutton, "Introduction: The Contours of Modern Caribbean Politics," in Anthony Payne and Paul Sutton (eds.), *Modern Caribbean Politics* (Baltimore: Johns Hopkins University Press, 1993), 25.

30. A. N. R. Robinson, "The West Indies Beyond 1992," a paper cited in West Indian Commission, *Time for Action: The Report of the West Indian Commission* (Black Rock, Barbados: The West Indian Commission, 1992), 3.

31. Richard J. Bloomfield, "Making the Western Hemisphere Safe for Democracy? The OAS Defense-of-Democracy Regime," in Kaysen, Pastor, and Reed (eds.), *Collective Responses to Regional Problems,* 20.

32. For an elaborate discussion of the obstacles that have surfaced since the end of the cold war, see Griffith, *The Quest for Security in the Caribbean,* chap. 6.

33. Sandiford, quoted in Griffith, *The Quest for Security in the Caribbean,* 149.

34. See, for example, the extensive definitional undertaking in Peter R. Odell, "The Caribbean and the Outside World: Geopolitical Considerations," in Emanuel de Kadt (ed.), *Patterns of Foreign Influence in the Caribbean* (London: Oxford University Press, 1972), 18–19.

35. Knight, *The Caribbean,* xv.

36. Richard E. Feinberg, "Introduction and Overview," in Richard E. Feinberg (ed.), *Central America: International Dimensions of the Crisis* (New York: Holmes and Meier, 1982), 1. In the same source, see chapters 8 and 9 for analyses of the roles played by European parties and the Catholic Church.

37. Griffith, *The Quest for Security in the Caribbean,* 258.

38. West Indian Commission, *Time for Action,,* 576–92.

39. West Indian Commission, *Time for Action,* 519.

40. For a discussion of the links between the education and skills of Caribbean publics and the regions orientation toward democratic institutions, see Franklin W. Knight, "The Societies of the Caribbean Since Independence," in Jorge I. Dominguez, Robert A. Pastor, and R. Delisle Worrell (eds.), *Democracy in the Caribbean: Political, Economic, and Social Perspectives* (Baltimore: Johns Hopkins University Press, 1993), 29–41.

41. Carl Stone, quoted in Griffith, *The Quest for Security in the Caribbean*, 248. A similar theme can be found in Ramesh Ramsaran, *The Commonwealth Caribbean in the World Economy* (London: Macmillan, 1989).

42. Kalman H. Silvert, "The Caribbean and North America," in Tad Szulc (ed.), *The United States and the Caribbean* (Englewood Cliffs, N. J.: Prentice-Hall, 1971), 195.

3

THE STATE OF THE REGION

Trends Affecting the Future of Caribbean Security

ANTHONY T. BRYAN

The major political and economic challenges facing the Caribbean as we approach the twenty-first century have been discussed in several recent general studies and a productive dialogue among scholars and policy makers has ensued.[1] Discussions on the state of security, always a major concern for the Caribbean region, have gone through an interesting evolution in the post-cold war period, namely, the emphasis on the strong links between the range of development and security concerns.

For example, the topic of small state security was one of the major worries of Caribbean scholars during the 1970s and 1980s, while the Cold War was still germane. The topic had both domestic and international facets. Its major themes (geopolitics, militarization, external intervention, subregional imperialism, domestic and regional instability, peace and development) were eventually categorized under the broader rubric of "vulnerability." The threats to economic security identified then involved "action that can have the effect of undermining a state's economic welfare and which, additionally, can also be used as an instrument of political interference."[2] The argument was framed in the prevailing economic and development models of the period, which included protected domestic and regional markets, bilateral and multilateral concessionary aid, and commodity price stabilization, and did not foresee the challenges that would emerge as a result of the completion of structural adjustment, the process of liberalization of the global economy, and the implementation of new trading blocs. Today, the vulnerability of Caribbean states has increased, and the challenges to economic security, as well as its political consequences, are now receiving additional emphasis. This chapter looks at trends in the following areas: political economy and development strategy; democracy and governance; economic integration and free trade: transnational issues, such as drug trafficking and migration; and the Caribbean's new international role.

TRENDS IN THE POLITICAL ECONOMY OF THE CARIBBEAN

The structural adjustment and reforms carried out by several Caribbean countries since the mid–1980s were not willingly implemented nor sustained by domestic political constituencies. For the most part, such changes in the macroeconomic environment were mandated by international financial or donor institutions and implemented by reform-minded governments or by governments that saw no alternative. As a general proposition, liberalization of the economy should be delayed until good fiscal policies can be put into place. Macroeconomic stability is essential to maintain the reforms and to allow incentive policies for domestic public and private investment, as well as foreign direct investment (FDI) to work.[3] But this sequence has been a challenge for small open Caribbean economies that are vulnerable to large external shocks and find it difficult to carry sufficient reserves, maintain adequate borrowing capacity, and encourage proper exchange rate policies.

In general, the present transition in the political economy of the Caribbean region is full of uncertainties. Liberalization and privatization policies have been portrayed by some politicians as being growth-inducing, when in effect they are not. Undertaking such reforms encounters resistance and costs. Also, individual countries need to weigh the immediate costs of free trade because among other negative impacts, trade liberalization, far from leading to greater exports, can provoke macroeconomic disequilibrium with commensurate rises in unemployment and underemployment rates.

Concerns for alleviating poverty and income equality caused by the reforms have not been fully integrated into proposals for growth. Many of the Caribbean's smaller economies are heavily dependent upon one (or a few) traditional export commodities for which world prices are not likely to rise. Increased crime, diminishing social support services, and dramatic increases in the poverty index (already quite visible even in relatively prosperous societies such as Trinidad and Tobago and Barbados) constitute major negative impacts of the reforms. In many Caribbean and Latin American countries, the much-heralded free market economic reforms have produced their own immediate Waterloo—benefits for a few, uncertainty for many, and the further impoverishment of the masses through the fiscal inability of governments to maintain essential social and infrastructural services. Much more has to be done domestically to compensate the losers.

CARIBBEAN DEMOCRACY AND GOVERNANCE

Certain issues of governance have emerged with the changes in political economy. Attempted coups d'état in Trinidad and Tobago in 1990 and in Venezuela in 1992, as well as the current political transition in Haiti, indicate that strengthening democracy is one of the major items on the immediate security agenda. There is widespread official and public perception in the region that economic vulnerability is at the core of Caribbean insecurity. Instability will increase if the economic pillars that support democratic regimes are eroded. Caribbean democratic and internal security also are under attack by the opportunities created or condoned for drug traffickers, arms smugglers, and money launderers to operate. In some states, such as Trinidad and Tobago, Guyana, and Haiti, ethnic and class tensions may worsen if economic circumstances deteriorate and political factions exploit the situation. The current situations in two of the Caribbean's largest nations, Cuba and Haiti, are indicative of some specific and complex issues in the process of democracy and governance. While even in the Caribbean's strongest democracies, new factors have conspired to challenge deeply held traditions.

Cuba

In contrast to the English-speaking Caribbean countries, which are still strongly democratic, Cuba is laboring under a discredited ideological model that does not encourage democracy. Both the U. S. embargo of Cuba and the outdated communist regime of Fidel Castro are post–Cold War relics. Relations between Cuba and the United States have worsened since President Bill Clinton signed into law on March 12, 1996, the "Cuban Liberty and Democratic Solidarity Act" (popularly known as the Helms-Burton Act), which is intended to make the embargo against Cuba broader and tighter and to encourage democracy in Cuba. Strong criticism of the legislation by the allies of the United States, particularly Canada and the

European Union, as well as the latter's approval of its own legislation in November 1996 to retaliate against any U. S. action, suggests that Cuba's future is once more a global concern.

Concurrently, relations between Cuba and its neighbors in the Caribbean have accelerated.[4] Cuba is being included in future Caribbean integration scenarios. The eventual participation of Cuba as an open market economy in the Caribbean will have both trade-creating effects (for regional tourism and services) and trade-diverting effects (assembly industries, some agricultural exports) on other Caribbean countries. At present, Cuba's centralized economy, production costs for certain export commodities, expensive port charges, and a lack of regular transportation links to the southern Caribbean have been identified as impediments to an increase in Cuba's overall trade with its free-market Caribbean neighbors.[5] But this will change.

A restructured Cuba will produce short-term shifts in existing trade and investment patterns that will result in a revised set of comparative advantages in the region.[6] Economic and political reforms in Cuba, leading to an open economy and normalization of relations with the United States, will result in a massive increase in U. S.-Cuban trade, possible U. S. economic assistance, and vast improvement in the investment and tourism climates in Cuba. It also would mean greater Cuban and regional interdependence with the U. S. economy. In anticipation of an eventual free market and regionally competitive Cuba, other Caribbean countries are capitalizing on their niche advantages and positioning themselves as players with a substantial stake in the Cuban economy. The current rationale for other Caribbean governments and the regional private sector to increase ties with Cuba is based more on commercial possibilities and less on the government and politics of the Castro regime.

Haiti

Neither the political transition nor the full economic recovery of Haiti are imminent or certain. The road map to a democratic transition in Haiti is by no means precise. Haiti still lacks strong political and institutional bases for the maintenance of a democratic state. Elements of the old corrupt traditional political culture have not disappeared. Social justice and economic equality have yet to become major ingredients in the political and economic equations. The transition will be complete only when a clean break with the historic systems of social and political injustice is evident to the majority of the Haitian people.

Haiti also faces a number of challenges in its economic long-term development. While the international emergency assistance plan and the incentives offered to investors may provide an economic kick start, the daunting task of rebuilding the Haitian economy will depend not only on political stability but also on long-term improvements in the depressed social and physical infrastructure. Haiti also faces stiff competition for international trade and foreign investment from other Caribbean countries, such as Trinidad and Tobago and Jamaica, which have liberalized their economies and are globally competitive. At present, despite the democratic electoral transition in December 1995,[7] the Haitian people are restless and expecting miracles. In the best of times they have lived in various versions of a benign authoritarian state. Democracy is a new and untested condition.[8]

DEMOCRATIC TRADITIONS UNDER CHALLENGE

The countries of the Commonwealth Caribbean maintain some of the hemisphere's strongest democratic traditions. But even those countries with traditions of parliamentary democracy are vulnerable to terrorists, the corruption of law enforcement officials, and domestic insurrection. Even the much-heralded Westminster model of parliamentary government is susceptible to authoritarian dispensation in the absence of traditional safeguards and rules.

Several of the pillars that support democratic regimes are eroding. It is difficult to be complacent about the future of democracy, even in the English-speaking Caribbean countries. Freedom House surveys over the past twenty years have characterized that part of the Caribbean as one of the most developed zones of democracy in the world. The English-speaking Caribbean (Commonwealth Caribbean) region has been exceptional in the consistency of free and fair elections, the observation of political rights and civil liberties, competitive party systems, and the rule of law. The institutions, behavior, and cultural values have a deep tradition in the Commonwealth Caribbean. But until very recently, the same could not be said of a majority of the broader circum-Caribbean, including Latin American countries on the mainland of Central America.

Recent research in Jamaica and some other Commonwealth Caribbean countries reveals some troubling trends apparent since the 1980s, namely declining voter turnout, particularly among the youth, and sharp declines in public interest in parliamentary proceedings.[9] Such voter alienation could eventually strengthen the emergence of single-party rule and perpetuate the financial and organizational advantages of dominant parties. Similarly, failure to invest constantly (because of budgetary constraints or lack of foreign assistance) in institutions such as the legal systems and mechanisms for public security is placing severe strains on democratic governance.

THE OVEREXTENDED STATE

A concurrent trend is the inability of the state (during circumstances of considerable downsizing and economic liberalization) to deliver levels of welfare and social services, similar to the last three decades. This can be viewed as being partially responsible for the erosion of its effectiveness and the questioning of its legitimacy. The great dilemma is the collapse of the overextended state and the pressure on regimes to provide economic support and deliver social services more rapidly and efficiently, even while their capacity to do so is severely diminished.

But that is only part of the story. The managerial capacity of the state in some countries is in shambles and needs to be rebuilt in order to deliver public services and confront the challenges created by a competitive market economy. On the *political* side, choices are not easy. In their attempts to meet these demands, and because of the technical stress of adjustment, stabilization, and liberalization measures, some governments have resorted to strong and unpopular action (and little public relations) to carry out reforms.[10] As a consequence, they have created some doubt about their loyalty to the democratic process. On the *economic* side, public tolerance for further sacrifice is also diminishing as the tasks of dismantling or restructuring state enterprises and financial systems continue. Obviously, antireformist coalitions spanning the political spectrum have great opportunities to manipulate public cynicism and fear. Some of the strongest antireform sentiments emanate from those who are not prepared to deal with a competitive market environment.

Future economic growth will in turn generate renewed debate over the role of the state. While the inflation rates and fiscal deficits are being contained in most Caribbean countries, and growth rates are respectable, the economic foundations are shaky. Revenues from privatization sales and reductions in basic government services are not formulas for sustainable growth.[11] Consequently, the fundamental issue of further reform remains in doubt.

POLITICAL PARTIES: NEW IDENTITIES

Declining access to scarce economic largesse, spectacles of corruption in government, abuses of political power, and the use of declining public funds to reward the ruling party faithful have severely weakened traditional political parties in the Commonwealth Caribbean. Many have also lost their historical and ideological differences. As one political observer has noted, "Typically, the political party, whatever the label, is now a multi-class coalition, funded largely by big business interests, led by the middle class and seeking to sustain popular electoral support with declining resources."[12]

The perception in the present climate of the inability to gain redress of grievance through the existing parliamentary system has been identified as one of the reasons for the attempted coup d'état by the Muslimeen in Trinidad and Tobago in 1990.[13]

LEADERSHIP CHANGES

Newer technocratic governments and younger and perhaps less charismatic leadership is likely to emerge for the remainder of the 1990s. Caribbean electorates are demanding more accountability and clearer economic programs from their leaders, who seem increasingly like pragmatic technocrats. This change is driven by public anger at failing economies, rising social ills, and endemic corruption. Structural adjustment programs also are producing tensions and dysfunctions in society.[14]

Changes in regional leadership also coincide with the emergence of a new global political and economic order. Some elder statesmen such as Michael Manley of Jamaica and Cheddi Jagan of Guyana (both now deceased) pragmatically dispensed with their socialist labels and moved their countries sharply toward free market economies. Cuba's Fidel Castro has resisted such dramatic change and has introduced a curious brand of à la carte capitalism. Recent economic reforms have encouraged direct foreign investment in certain sectors of the Cuban economy and permitted the evolution of a small merchant class within the margins of the state-managed dollar economy.

BUSINESS, LABOR AND GOVERNMENT: NEW RELATIONSHIPS

In many countries of the Caribbean, the private sector is now regarded as the catalyst for economic growth. The privatization process itself has moved business into a more autonomous political and economic relationship with the state. Ironically, private control of the media, certain education sectors, and worker training has also increased private sector responsibility for legitimizing the social order and attending to public welfare. The rise of business has been met by a commensurate decline in labor unions. It is labor that has carried most of the costs of structural adjustment and reform, and labor unions themselves are being weakened by a new cooperative spirit between business and government. Consequently, there is a substantial agenda for labor market reforms requiring consensus rather than confrontation, as in the past.

In sum, the effects on the Caribbean democratic tradition of dramatic shifts in social and class structure, declining political participation, frustration with the parliamentary system of politics, changes in leadership, conversion to neoliberal economic policies by political parties that have traditionally represented labor, and changing relationships between labor, business, and government are yet to become apparent.

ECONOMIC INTEGRATION AND FREE TRADE

Today, prospects for free trade in the Americas are hopeful. In the last few years, most Latin American and Caribbean nations experienced the retreat from consummate protectionism and statism and the advance toward market economies and trade liberalization. The North American Free Trade Agreement (NAFTA) validated the logic of the international trade agenda and the cross-border business realities already existing in the hemisphere. The decision of the Summit of the Americas in December 1994 to move toward a Free Trade Area of the Americas (FTAA) by 2005 has made the long-term objective of trade and economic integration in the Western Hemisphere a real possibility.

The new integration process in the Western Hemisphere goes beyond the traditional concept of countries simply extending reciprocal trade preferences to their trading partners. The process has five elements: the liberalization of barriers to trade in goods and services; the elimination of restraints on investments; the provision of free labor movement for specialized workers; harmonization of tax and monetary policies; and the establishment of supraregional institutions to administer the arrangements and to engage in dispute resolution. Notable progress has been made in Latin America and the Caribbean in liberalizing trade in goods and services and in building supraregional institutions, but coordination of monetary and fiscal policies has not really advanced.[15]

A functioning Free Trade Area of the Americas is a long-term undertaking, and subregional free trade agreements (FTAs) can help promote the objective. Latin American and Caribbean countries are proceeding at a rapid rate with their own subregional integration efforts. Many of the FTAs being negotiated between subregions are overlapping and may eventually create layers of bureaucratic procedures for enforcement, as well as obstacles to liberalization beyond their borders. However, once the various subregional arrangements continue to lower their barriers against imports from other countries, and their associations remain open to other countries willing to join on the same terms, they may be regarded more as building blocks and not as stumbling blocks in the movement toward greater regional integration. In this scenario, it seems almost certain that NAFTA discipline will not be weakened and that other countries in the hemisphere will have to undertake the obligations required by NAFTA in non-trade issues such as the environment, labor standards, democracy, and human rights.

While there is a strong rationale for some Caribbean countries to enter NAFTA, either individually, through the fifteen-member Caribbean Community (CARICOM) grouping, or collectively, as nations of the Caribbean Basin Initiative (CBI), interim arrangements are necessary for those countries that are unable to undertake even the present NAFTA discipline. The static estimates of the impact of NAFTA on Caribbean countries indicate that without interim parity it will have a strong impact on some of the countries with export concentration on North America. Passage of an interim trade parity program or CBI enhancement legislation in the U. S. legislature would facilitate the process.

Similarly, while this emerging hemispheric trade policy toward the FTAA is positive, it presents special problems for some Caribbean countries. Absolute reciprocity may be the ultimate goal of hemispheric trade liberalization, but some smaller Caribbean economies simply cannot compete with countries having more developed productive structures and a range of available technologies. They cannot offer absolute reciprocity to industrialized countries, at least in the short run, and some compromise on the part of the developed trade partners is essential. In addition, most individual countries in the wider Caribbean region are not yet prepared to subscribe to the required trade disciplines.

Another reality is that the countries of the wider Caribbean are not at the same stages of development, and it is probable that their paths will diverge even further in the future. Each country will reserve the option to decide whether its free trade objectives are served best by pursuing a subregional or individual country approach. Caribbean countries also will continue to be proactive in overcoming the disadvantages of size through wider subregional trade and integration schemes, such as the newly formed (1994) twenty-five nation Association of Caribbean States (ACS).[16] Eventually, a strong subregional grouping such as CARICOM would be in a better position to negotiate. Indeed, all member countries have agreed to establish a high-level negotiating team drawn from national governments and regional institutions to negotiate NAFTA parity for Caribbean Basin nations, the FTAA, matters relating to the European Union (EU) and the Lomé IV Convention. A "draft model agreement" has been crafted that seeks to address the division within CARICOM between larger nations (such as Trinidad and Tobago, and Jamaica), which are expanding their markets through agreements outside CARICOM, and the smaller nations, which are reluctant to do so.[17] But joint action does not necessarily mean the simultaneous movement of all members of the group. Despite the logic of strong subregional grouping, some governments in the Caribbean will have to allow themselves the flexibility to proceed at different speeds and in different ways to an FTAA.

THE SMALLER ECONOMIES

In general, governments and business entities in the smaller Caribbean Community countries have mixed feelings about the free trade trend. Most of these countries, members of the subregional grouping of the Organization of Eastern Caribbean States (OECS), have undiversified economies, based on a few primary commodities or services (such as tourism). In St. Lucia and Dominica, bananas accounted for almost half of merchandise exports in 1994. Preferential treatment for their bananas in the EU is under strong legal challenge by Central American growers in collusion with the United States. Similarly, some manufacturers fear that their products will be cast aside by an influx of global imports. Clearly, these smaller economies are more de-pendent on foreign trade for their fiscal revenues than are some of their larger Caribbean and Latin American neighbors. They also maintain a lower percentage of international reserves. Consequently, a strong dependence on external financing, a more liberalized trade system, and a concentrated and vulnerable export structure would pose greater external risks for them. Some may also argue that the high costs of adjustment for the FTAA will be immediate, but the rewards will be realized only in the longer term. Even-tually, some countries may not survive the wait.

MEETING THE CHALLENGES

The CARICOM response to these challenges on the trade horizon include the imminent creation of a single market and economy (SM&E) to facilitate the economic development of member states through provisions such as the unrestricted movement of goods, services, capital and labor, and peo-ple. However, the challenges from the FTAA, from Europe, and from within the diversity of Caricom itself all place the SM&E under significant stress. The SM&E is still too small to develop the economies of scale nec-essary for global penetration. Furthermore, the Common External Tariff, which is part of the SM&E, will be overtaken by the General Agreement on Tariffs and Trade (GATT) and the FTAA. Policy convergence is necessary for a functioning common market, but the domestic policies of some of the members of CARICOM depend on the liberalization of markets and the increasing mobility of productive factors. The potential for integrating investment and production within the SM&E is limited.[18]

There is a positive side to the picture. Trying to meet the demands of the FTAA process will lead CARICOM countries to also meet the criteria for global integration. These include long-term strategic planning, market diversification, stronger institutional capacity, and efficient marketing. Although the concerns of the smaller economies are logical, arguments in favor of eventual free trade are also strong. Preparations for hemispheric free trade should be seen as part of a process of erecting a framework to move Caribbean countries from protected inward-looking arrangements to a system that will improve their chances in dynamic global markets, in the Western Hemisphere, Western Europe, Asia, or elsewhere. Unfortunately, some countries may be moving too slowly to prepare themselves for the FTAA.

In sum, in the short and medium term, the Caribbean's broader strategy for trade and integration is likely to have the following elements: negotiate and implement a process for phased accession to NAFTA, including docking and parity arrangements; determine the weight to be afforded to relations with Europe in light of what will in all probability be a very different successor arrangement to Lomé IV; come to terms with a Lomé/NAFTA/GATT relationship that presumes reciprocity without totally disrupting the economic, social, and political fabric of small island states; determine how integration efforts within the wider Caribbean region can be of best use in its strategy toward the United States and Europe; complete the process of liberalizing and deregulating regional economies to move toward the FTAA and take advantage of the emerging global economic order.

In the long term, the only path by which the Caribbean can avoid economic marginalization and achieve advantageous or reasonably equitable relationships with North America, the Western Hemisphere, and Europe, is through strategies to capture the benefits of market size and energize the potential negotiating strategy of the wider Caribbean.

THE "DOWNSIDE" OF LIBERALIZATION

The liberalization of economies and the evolving financial markets in the Caribbean may be a welcome and legitimate development. But there is an enormous "downside" to this process of trade and financial liberalization. Without effective controls and safeguards, the economies of these small states are susceptible to a range of new vulnerabilities. Clearly, corruption at all levels is a very disturbing trend.

The reputations of certain Caribbean countries already have been hurt by the establishment of offshore havens, including so-called B-Banks or file folder banks, which are used to carry on fraud or legitimate business. No region of the world has a greater concentration of offshore secrecy financial havens than the Caribbean. Given the globalization of finance and investment, there may be a need for these centers. But their use by organized crime and money launderers has dangerous implications for Caribbean countries. The Caribbean's location as an important link in the distribution and transhipment chain of narco-trafficking that integrates Bolivia, Peru, and Colombia on the one hand, and the Caribbean and North Atlantic on the other, makes it an attractive region for money launderers. Neither traditional theories of political relations, distinct cultural characteristics, nor poverty can fully explain the money laundering phenomenon. The islands with the largest offshore centers are the most European of all—in culture, law, and business traditions. They are not destitute, and they benefit from transfers from the metropolis. Perhaps an explanation lies in "enterprise theory," where economic activity takes place across a spectrum of businesses that is both legitimate and illegitimate. Decisions to open offshore havens that ensure secrecy are rational business decisions.

Unfortunately, the social, economic, and political impact of the "money laundering" phenomenon is not restricted to major financial or offshore centers, or to the reputation of some countries for confidentiality laws. The opening of markets and financial liberalization in Caribbean countries provides opportunities for legitimate investors and businessmen, as well as criminals! The spectacle of business monopolies controlled by criminal elements can constrain investment and competitiveness in a country, while massive infusions of illegal funds into the economy can have an adverse effect through the artificial inflation of prices. In some cases, the launderers simply buy banks, or non-bank financial institutions, or gain corrupt influence over officials of local financial institutions in order to move their proceeds into the main financial streams.

Throughout the world, criminal groups control hundreds of billions of dollars in financial assets, and they move back and forth easily between legal and illegal activities. They exploit political instability and utilize the new communications technologies to their advantage. Organized crime at this level threatens the stability of global business and finance. It is a kind of "financial terrorism" that employs the computer keyboard. The possibility of being able to wreak financial havoc on small Caribbean states, if they become the focus of these operatives, is frightening enough. An even greater threat to Caribbean democratic institutions derives from the apparent increasing synergy between government officials and organized crime, including the drug cartels. Of similar concern is offshore computer

"on-line" casino gambling. Two Caribbean countries are under consideration as locations for this innovative, but perhaps illegal, form of cross-
border casino betting by computer, regarded as being in conflict with those
states in the United States that disallow casino gambling.[19]

For Caribbean countries, the distinctions between the legal and informal economy lie more in their "legal" character than in the "economic" nature of activities. Moreover, in countries with severe economic hardships,
laundered money can influence both the availability of foreign currency and
the stability of the exchange rate. The legitimate global financial community
does not take kindly to countries that knowingly facilitate laundering. There
is little incentive for foreign direct investment if the commercial sector is
dominated by criminals. Furthermore, countries such as the United States,
with extraterritorial reach in such matters, can have a devastating effect on
the financial sector of small countries that permit such activities. As the
Caribbean moves toward free trade and common markets, antilaundering
measures become more necessary. Legislation is in place in many Caribbean
countries for asset confiscation and other measures, but the record of implementation is unsatisfactory at best.[20] There are terrible costs to society, polity,
and economy associated with inaction in this circumstance.

TRANSNATIONAL ISSUES

Drug Trafficking

Increasingly, the major contributor to corruption and criminality in the region is drug trafficking. Some Eastern Caribbean countries on the northern
tier of South America have now become key transshipment routes for
South American cocaine into the U. S. and European markets. Most Caribbean countries cooperate with the United States in counternarcotics
efforts. Some recent U. S. antidrug action appeared to push extraterritorial
jurisdiction too far and provoked government and public hostility in some
Caribbean countries where the United States is perceived to breach
national sovereignty. A case in point is the United States Maritime and
Overflight (Ship Riders) Agreement, which is intended to stem the intraregional flow of drugs. The Agreement permits land and sea patrols by
U. S. Coast Guard and Navy vessels, maritime searches, and seizures and
arrests by U. S. law enforcement authorities within the national boundaries of Caribbean countries. It also allows U. S. aircraft to overfly Caribbean countries and order suspect aircraft to land there. Most Caribbean
countries have signed different versions of the Agreement, but its ability to
have any impact at all remains to be seen.[21]

Most Caribbean leaders are quite upset at the manner in which the United States is attempting to stem the flow of drugs through the region. They do not dispute the urgency of controlling the illegal traffic but resent U. S. pressure over how to fight the trade. They see it as unacceptable for the United States to bully weaker countries of limited resources into treaties and concessions without providing anything in return. Caribbean leaders are concerned that the United States is obsessed with the drug war but pays scant attention to other urgent regional issues. They want some concessions from the United States which trimmed aid to the region from $225 million in 1985 to $26 million in 1996. They have little capacity to deal with drug smugglers, but feel very maligned by the United States. So the policy dilemma for small Caribbean countries is that while even collectively they cannot stem the drug trade, the current anti-drug strategies of the United States threaten to impinge on the national sovereignty and the independent legal systems of those countries.

The transnational nature of the drug trade is difficult to combat. Narcotics trafficking is unlikely to stop in the near term, given the demand in the developed countries, the ease of electronic money laundering, offshore bank secrecy, a network of official protection enjoyed by traffickers, and the "corporate" structure of the drug trade. A new policy may be required—one that chases the money rather than the drugs.

The classic wider Caribbean example of an emerging "narco-economy" is Colombia. The country's economic liberalization program—or apertura—has made it very profitable for the drug kingpins to keep their financial resources in the country and inadvertently invest in their country's future economic development. Economists estimate that some $3 to $4 billion in profits derived from the illegal narcotics trade flows to Colombia annually. This sum accounts for 7 percent of the country's gross domestic product (GDP). Colombia's economic landscape has been infiltrated by drug money going into the import of consumer goods for cheap retail, large-scale commercial construction, local financial and securities markets, and newly privatized banks.

But the boom is not necessarily to Colombia's overall benefit. In fact, it is starting to backfire, as oversupply produces a recession in the construction industry; the sale of cut rate imports hurts small businessmen and even the giants of Colombian industry; and overvaluation of the peso produced by excessive liquidity in the financial system and loans for excessive consumption encourages more inflation. The unfortunate results are that foreign investors now shy away from Colombia; and capital flight of about $1.5 billion per year continues, as legitimate businesspeople try to move their assets abroad.[22]

Drug trafficking and the production of illegal narcotics is a security problem for Caribbean nations, but it also is a symptom of profound economic crisis. The failure of economic development strategies and the lack of viable economic alternatives have made the illegal narcotics business the most profitable sector of the Caribbean's informal economy. Domestic abuse and consumption of marijuana, heroin, and crack cocaine are now a serious threat to human development and social well-being in these nations. The domestic collateral damage produced by the drug trade is a danger to democracy.

One important goal in the international fight against drugs should be to support democratic institutions and combat efforts by drug cartels or other organized criminal groups to corrupt and penetrate democratic governments. Victory in the struggle against drugs is unlikely until those running the criminal organizations and cartels are put out of business. Otherwise, seized drugs and lost revenues are simply the cost of doing business. Given the region's limited resources, the drug trade will not be halted any time soon. In the meantime, corruption and violence will probably increase even more, and valuable national and regional resources will be diverted from infrastructure, education, and health care to fight the drug scourge.

Migration

The security issues related to international migration are problematic. Migration and international economic interdependence, and the economic, trade, and foreign investment consequences of migration (for both the sending and receiving societies) have emerged as major issues in international relations. The flood of Haitian refugees to the United States after the 1991 coup illustrates the extent of the problem. Haiti is an extreme example of Caribbean demographics. Under current conditions, the land can no longer adequately support its population. Many of Haiti's economic problems stem largely from an environmental crisis—the degradation of natural resources, made worse by the uncertainty of politics, development planning, and inadequate distribution and delivery systems. The depletion of resources is a fundamental cause of conflict, and human misery and national policies must make sustainable development a priority.

Haiti and Cuba (for other reasons) may be extreme scenarios of migration and refugees propelled by combinations of political and economic circumstances. However, migration, legal or illegal, will continue as a safety valve for economic dislocation in the Caribbean, and the resulting brain drain does not necessarily present a doomsday scenario for either the Caribbean or receiving countries such as the United States. The remittances and investments sent by productive Caribbean emigrants should be regarded as part of a larger transborder contribution to long-term economic growth, peace, and security in the hemisphere. Migration is actually an item on the international development agenda. Cross-border networks and linkages between diaspora and home societies will continue to sustain transborder migration flows. In spite of the current anti-immigration fervor, the United States, like other developed nations, stands to benefit economically from the immigration flows. The current restrictionist mood may slow down cross-border migration flows. However, in the near-to-medium term, it will more likely have the impact of entrenching some hardworking immigrants from the wider Caribbean into a perpetual underclass. This could create another type of economic security problem for the United States and Canada.

A NEW INTERNATIONAL ROLE

The Environment

Environmental concerns and issues of sustainable development are assuming increasing importance to the Caribbean. They are in fact critical to the economic survival of many countries. The environment is at the center of the tourism industry, the principal source of revenue for many countries, and coordination in the tourism sector inevitably implies coordination in the area of the environment. The urgency for effective disaster emergency response (witness 1995, the most destructive hurricane season in the Eastern Caribbean), storm hazard assessment and impact monitoring, disaster preparedness and prevention, relevant insurance, environmental health, and population relocation are some of the urgent matters that dictate consensus and collaboration at the regional and international levels.

At another level, the rapid industrialization of a major Caribbean country, Trinidad and Tobago provides a case study in the inherent risk for environmental disaster in a small country. Trinidad and Tobago is a hydrocarbon-based economy. In 1990, the hydrocarbon sector accounted for 31 percent of the GDP, 67 percent of exports, and 47 percent of government revenue. By the end of 1995, the country had become the major energy-based economy in the Caribbean, with major new investments (since 1993) of U. S. $3 billion into that sector. Heavy manufacturing activities include sugar refining, oil refining, and the production of ammonia, methanol, urea, direct reduced iron, steel, and cement.

The oil boom of the 1970s transformed Trinidad and Tobago from a fundamentally agricultural-oriented economy to a developing industrialized economy. This transformation continued rapidly, primarily due to the vast resources of relatively cheap natural gas. The World Bank has listed the number of industrial manufacturing establishments in Trinidad and Tobago as 643 in 1987, rising to 1,220 in 1990. It is estimated that in the year 2000, there will be over 3,100 industrial establishments within the 1,980 square miles of the nation's territory.

Unfortunately, the necessary associated environmental planning of an industrialization of this magnitude was never adequately performed. A lack of environmental consciousness and awareness in every stratum of society has resulted in a large majority of industries discharging unmonitored, untreated quantities of waste into the environment.[23]

In reality, Caribbean governments will need to overcome their ambivalence regarding environmental issues. Government, in collaboration with the private sector and NGOs as advocates, must develop regional strategies and set up effective mechanisms and infrastructure to regulate and enforce appropriate laws.[24]

MULTILATERAL MECHANISMS

The Caribbean can be described as the only region in the world that harbors such a diversity of political, administrative, and institutional systems in such a small geographical space, and for a relatively small population. Historical fragmentation into Spanish, English, French, Dutch, and more recently, American systems of politics and governance, testify to the plurality of possible constraints placed on collaboration in the multilateral arena. But difficult situations do not necessarily mean a lack of solutions. Indeed, if local or regional imperatives for collaboration do not prevail, international and hemispheric circumstances will dictate other responses.

Recent events in Haiti serve as an example of how the internal abuse of democracy and justice in one country can impact on, not only its own economic and entire developmental ethos, but also on the stability and security of the region. The concerted and measured diplomatic and military response of CARICOM and other Caribbean nations to these events subsequently had an impact on both the hemispheric body (the OAS) and the United Nations. The situation was sufficiently serious to solicit widespread international collaboration. But it was only as a 'regional' collective that the Caribbean could play its part in any significant way.

A new international role for Caribbean nations will take into account their participation in multilateral missions. Caribbean people have participated in election observer missions, and the region's police and defense forces have been involved in international monitoring and security missions. The CARICOM countries, with their traditions of parliamentary democracy and well-established professionalism in civil services and police and military forces, are well-poised to play active roles as trainers and observers in the international promotion of democracy worldwide. Such roles are subject to the economic limitations placed on small states. But with financial support from the UN or the OAS, Caribbean nations could become more actively involved in addressing international problems. Indeed, the formation of the ACS offers an opportunity for the extension of collaboration, both qualitatively and geographically, for a multilateral Caribbean impact on the promotion and enhancement of good governance, democracy, human rights, and justice in the region.

CONCLUSION

The global economic environment is in a state of rapid transition. The new dispensation in both the developing and the developed world is the opening up of national and regional economies to market forces. Profound transformations in relations among state, civil society, and economy are accompanying the process. In this vaguely Darwinian scenario, concepts of nationhood are being challenged by international integration, and national governments and politicians are hard-pressed to demonstrate proper administrative capacity over this implicit surrender of sovereignty. The Caribbean countries have to cope with these new dynamics; there are no precise road maps, no easy solutions—only operational principles.

Integration into the global economy is the best route for Caribbean countries. Free trade is inevitable. Economic marginalization would be one of the major security threats. While larger countries are not tolerant of exceptions from the new trading rules for smaller countries, a weaning period to adjust to new arrangements can be negotiated. In addition, Caribbean countries have to turn their attention to forging economic development strategies that go well beyond the current global euphoria with liberalization and privatization. In undertaking this task, CARICOM countries in particular have an advantage in respect of human capital. High literacy rates and excellent records of primary and secondary school enrollment must now be bolstered by proper policies to raise educational quality in technologies, management, and finance, which are crucial ingredients for competition in the emerging global economy.

The challenges are complex, but they all lead to eventual global interaction. Caribbean countries need to reposition their economies to take advantage of the transitions in the global economy. The NAFTA, the GATT, and negotiations for the FTAA provide them with a new scope to improve their trade and growth prospects. Preliminary studies suggest that many Caribbean countries could have a comparative advantage in the trade in services sector, primarily the provision of health care, biotechnology, tourism, education, finance, retirement, and information processing. But they need to move quickly to develop niches and progress beyond the stage of simply exporting manufactured goods. Services are increasing more rapidly as a component of international trade than is the export of manufactured goods.[25] This repositioning should not mean the abandonment of traditional sectors of the economy, such as manufacturing or agriculture; rather, it should include, if possible, the reform and strengthening of these sectors for global competitiveness.

The public and private sectors in the Caribbean will have to work in tandem to secure capital, technology, and marketing through joint ventures and strategic corporate alliances. Similarly, every effort will have to be made to repatriate or engage the talent of Caribbean human resources resident outside of the region. The forward-looking planners should already anticipate that the Caribbean's demography has expanded to include significant financial, intellectual, and market sectors among Caribbean peoples in Florida, New York, Toronto, London, and many other European and Latin American capitals.

In general, many of the trends outlined in this chapter have important implications for the security of the Caribbean region. Similarly, political polarization, ethnic and class tensions, environmental degradation (including oil spills and hazardous waste dumping), and food security also are "grey area" concerns for the future of Caribbean security. They form as much a part of the agenda for discussion as do security mechanisms, regional international regimes, or notions of "cooperative security."

Caribbean nations must be responsible for their own security. Some issues can be addressed on a national or a regional basis; others will have to be tackled through bilateral mechanisms; and yet others will require a global approach. Caribbean security issues for the rest of the 1990s will be complex and, in most cases, interrelated.

Most important, as this analysis suggests, there is a strong link between development concerns and security issues. Policies that enhance economic development, show distributive justice, encourage the rule of law, protect fundamental human rights, and foster the growth of democratic institutions also are security policies.

NOTES

1. Georges A. Fauriol and G. Philip Hughes (eds.), *U. S.–Caribbean Relations into the 21st Century* (Washington, D. C.: CSIS Americas Program, 1995) Policy Paper on the Americas, vol. VI, Study 4; Jorge Domínguez, "The Caribbean in a New International Context: Are Freedom and Peace a Threat to Its Security?" in Anthony T. Bryan (ed.), *The Caribbean: New Dynamics in Trade and Political Economy* (New Brunswick, N. J.: Transaction Publishers/North-South Center, 1995); Anthony T. Bryan, *The Caribbean: New Dimensions in Trade and Political Economy* (New Brunswick, N. J.: Transactions Publishers/North-South Center, 1995); Anthony P. Maingot, "Trends in U. S.–Caribbean Relations," *The Annals of the American Academy of Political and Social Science*, vol. 533 (May 1994); Hilbourne A. Watson (ed.), *The Caribbean in the Global Political Economy* (Boulder and London: Lynne Rienner Publishers, 1994); Andrés Serbin and Anthony T. Bryan (eds.), *El Caribe Hacia el 2000* (Caracas: Editorial Nueva Sociedad, 1991).

2. Commonwealth Secretariat, *Vulnerability: Small States*, 23, 112–13.

3. Lawrence H. Summers and Vinod Thomas, "Recent Lessons of Development," *The World Bank Research Observer*, vol. 8, no. 2 (1993), 241–54.

4. For an analysis of this relationship, see Anthony T. Bryan, "Cuba and the Caribbean: A Reversal of Bad Fortune?" in Joseph Tulchin, Rafael Hernández, and Andrés Serbin, *Cuba and the Caribbean: Regional Issues and Trends in the Post-Cold War Era* (Wilmington, Del.: Scholarly Resources, 1997), 163–78.

5. Michael Becker, "Study says Caribbean–Cuba trade unlikely to grow." *Caribbean Week* (January 6–19, 1996); and Michael Becker, "Caribbean Nations Consider Free Trade Pact with Cuba." *The Miami Herald* (July 19, 1997).

6. Carmelo Mesa-Lago, *Are Economic Reforms Propelling Cuba to the Market?* (Coral Gables, Fla.: North-South Center, University of Miami, 1994); Ernest H. Preeg, *Cuba and the New Caribbean Economic Order* (Washington, D. C.: The Center for Strategic and International Studies, 1994).

7. As Howard J. Wiarda has warned, elections are but only one source of democratic legitimacy and one of several routes to power. Elections may simply convey tentative democratic legitimacy. See his "U. S. Policy and Democracy in the Caribbean and Latin America," *Policy Papers on the Americas*, vol. VI, Study 7, July, 21 1995 (Washington, D. C.: Center for Strategic and International Studies).

8. Anthony T. Bryan, "Haiti: Kick Starting the Economy," *Current History*, vol. 94, no. 589 (1995), 65–70. For analyses of the Haitian situation, see also Robert Maguire, "Demilitarizing Public Order in a Predatory

State: The Case of Haiti," *The North-South Agenda Paper No. 17* (Miami: North-South Center Press, University of Miami); Ernest H. Preeg, *The Haitian Dilemma: A Case Study in Demographics, Development, and U. S. Foreign Policy,* (Washington, D. C.: The Center for Strategic and International Studies, 1996); and Robert Maguire, Edwige Balutansky, Jacques Fomerand, Larry Minear, William G. O'Neill, Thomas G. Weiss and Sarah Zaidi, *Haiti Held Hostage: International Responses to the Quest for Nationhood, 1986 to 1996* (Providence, R. I.: Thomas J. Watson Jr. Institute for International Studies and the United Nations University, 1996), Occasional Paper No. 23.

9. See Patrick Emmanuel, *Governance and Democracy in the Commonwealth Caribbean: An Introduction* (Cave Hill, Barbados: Institute for Social and Economic Research, 1993).

10. For an excellent analysis of the policy and institutional pressures encountered by several governments in the trade reform process, see Sarath Rajapatirana, "Post Trade Liberalization Policy and Institutional Challenges in Latin America and the Caribbean." (Washington, D. C.: The World Bank, 1995), Mss.

11. A case in point is Trinidad and Tobago (a nation of 1.3 million people), which, because of its liberalized economy, had attracted U. S. $2 billion in foreign direct investment between 1992 and 1994 and had negotiated for a further U. S. $4 billion to be invested between 1996 and 1999. Most of this investment is committed to the country's newly privatized vibrant oil and energy sector, yet poverty continues to be an intractable problem, and the poor now comprise between 21 and 30 percent of the population. See Anthony T. Bryan, "Trinidad and Tobago: Dynamic Economy and New Politics," *North-South Focus,* (North-South Center, University of Miami), vol. V, no.1, 1996.

12. Trevor Munroe, "Democracy and Drugs in the Caribbean: Some Policy Perspectives," 1995 Mss. Paper presented at the Conference on International Narco-Trafficking on the Economy of Caribbean States. Institute of International Relations/University of the West Indies, Trinidad, January 19–21.

13. Leda Pérez, *The Trinity Divided: Ethnopolitics and Islamic Fundamentalism in Trinidad and Tobago.* (Miami: University of Miami, Graduate School of International Studies, 1996), Ph.D. dissertation, Mss.

14. For insights on the current dilemmas of Caribbean leadership, see the collection of essays in Joyce Hoebing (ed.) "Leadership in the Caribbean: Working Papers," *Policy Papers on the Americas,* vol. VII, Study 5, (Washington, D. C.: Center for Strategic and International Studies, 1996).

15. Gary Clyde Hufbauer and Jeffrey J. Schott, *Western Hemisphere Economic Integration* (Washington, D. C.: Institute for International Economics, 1994), 10–14.

16. Henry S. Gill, "The Association of Caribbean States: Prospects for a Quantum Leap?" *North-South Agenda Papers*, no. 11 (Miami: North-South Center Press/University of Miami, 1995).

17. See *Inside NAFTA*, vol.3, no. 22 (October 30, 1996), 4–5. One member of the group, Trinidad and Tobago, has submitted an application to join NAFTA in mid-1996 in advance of any regional approach.

18. See Anthony T. Bryan, "Going Global Cautiously: CARICOM and the OECS Face Free Trade," *Caricom PERSPECTIVE*, Issue No. 66 (June 1996), 29–31. For a detailed study of the trade challenges, options, and available strategies for the Caribbean, see Anthony T. Bryan, "Trading Places: The Caribbean Faces Europe and the Americas in the Twenty-First Century." *The North-South Agenda*, no 27 (Coral Gables, FL.: North South Center at the University of Miami, 1997).

19. *Miami Herald*, May 24, 1995.

20. For a discussion of money laundering countermeasures, see Ivelaw L. Griffith "The Money Laundering Dilemma in the Caribbean," *Cuaderno de Trabajo*, no. 4 (Rio Piedras, Puerto Rico: Institute of Caribbean Studies, 1995).

21. The scope of the drug-trafficking trade is discussed in the following: David A. Andelman, "The Economics of the Drug Trade," *U. S./Latin Trade: The Magazine of Trade and Investment in the Americas*, vol. 3, no. 9 (September 1995), 42–49: Cathy Booth, "Caribbean Blizzard," *Time* (February 26, 1996); Klaus de Albuquerque, "Drugs in the Caribbean: A Five Part Series," *Caribbean Week* (Barbados), various issues, (January–March 1996).

22. Michelle Celarier, "Finance in the Narco State," *Global Finance* (May 1995), 36–39.

23. On the industrialization of Trinidad and Tobago, see Bryan "Trinidad and Tobago: Dynamic Economy and New Politics."

24. See Erik Blommestein, Barbara Boland, Trevor Harker, Swinburne Lestrade, and Judith Towle "Sustainable Development and Small Island States of the Caribbean," in George A. Maul (ed.) *Small Islands: Marine Science and Sustainable Development* (Washington, D. C.: American Geophysical Union, 1996).

25. World Bank, "Caribbean Region: Coping with Changes in the External Environment," LAC 1281, April 1994. For one analysis of how the process of "global repositioning" can be undertaken, see Richard L. Bernal "Strategic Global Repositioning and Future Economic Development in Jamaica," *The North-South Agenda Papers*, no. 18, (Miami: North-South Center Press/ University of Miami, 1995).

4

GLOBALIZATION, REGIONALIZATION, AND CIVIL SOCIETY IN THE GREATER CARIBBEAN

ANDRÉS SERBIN

GENEALOGY OF THE CARIBBEAN BASIN: IN SEARCH OF A DEFINITION

Elsewhere, I have analyzed the various definitions that led to the identification of the Caribbean Basin as a distinctive region in the hemisphere, particularly as a region different from Latin America. Here, I will examine how these definitions have come into being, that is, the formulation of various definitions of the region in relation to the various states involved, including their many agendas, priorities, and interests:

1. a *geostrategic* definition, in terms of the Caribbean Basin, within the context of the bipolar confrontation that characterized the Cold War (a context including the Cuban Revolution, the processes of decolonization of the non-Spanish Caribbean and, subsequently, the Central American crisis), linked to the United States' security interests in the region, which resulted, during the '80s, in the Caribbean Basin Initiative (CBI), involving both the island countries of the region and several non-Communist countries of the Central American isthmus. This perspective, clearly identified with the realist approach to international-relations theory, assigned priority to the strategic-military challenge posed by Cuban-Soviet influence of the region to the United States' interests;

2. an *ethnohistorical* definition, emphasizing the decolonization and post-colonial consolidation of the non-Spanish-speaking Caribbean and stressing the common historical experience molded by the plantation economy, slavery, and the incorporation of contingents of African origin into the populations of the Caribbean islands and the Guianas and Belize. This approach was useful for differentiating the region from the former European metropolises and the United States, on the one hand, and the continental neighbors of Latin America, on the other;

3. a *Third World* definition of the Caribbean Basin, influenced by attempts on the part of the developing countries to promote a New World Economic Order (NWEO), emphasizing the community of interests of those countries (and of the South in general) facing the industrialized countries of the North, as well as the possibilities of South-South cooperation. This definition includes the island countries of the Antilles, the Central American countries, and the so-called "regional powers" of the 1970s: Cuba, Mexico, Venezuela and Colombia. The clearest expression of this view was probably the creation of the Latin American Economic System (SELA) in 1975, with the participation of the aforementioned countries along with the other South American countries and with the explicit exclusion of the United States. In this perspective, priority is assigned to regional convergence regarding socioeconomic development.

By and large, these definitions structured the thinking of political elites (and some intellectuals) in the region; often, they accorded a leading role to the more powerful regional and extra-regional states. Hence, the dominant definition of the *Caribbean Basin* gave priority to strategic security in line with the national interests of the United States, while the other definitions took more account of the self-determination and autonomy of the states of the region and placed greater emphasis on political economy or culture. In turn, economic and entrepreneurial elites, both regional and extra-regional, saw the region's identity in terms of national and regional markets for trade and investment limited by national and subregional regulations, particularly within the framework of the CBI.

This genealogy of the regional identifications prevailing until the '80s is currently challenged by the new global, hemispheric, and regional conditions following the dissolution of the Communist bloc and the end of the Cold War, which has substantially modified the international environment of the region. Particularly since the triggering of the "external debt crisis" and the advent of bipolarity, the international environment is shaped more and more by the global political economy.[1]

THE GLOBAL CHALLENGES AND THE REGION

Economic Globalization

The economic transformations of the international system are based on three fundamental processes: financial globalization (with the transnationalization of investment and the transnational flow of capital); the information revolution; and the restructuring of production from the Fordist/Taylorist model to the more flexible Toyotist or post-Fordist model.[2] But globalization also has sociopolitical dimensions (e.g., the redefinition of the state in accordance with market dynamics and the consequent global furtherance of Western democracy and cultural dimensions (e.g., the spread of Western consumerism and the undermining of local values and identity).[3]

Following the collapse of the Bretton Woods system, the globalization of the financial markets accelerated, leading to a significant increase in the transnational flow of capital. Nevertheless, as pointed out by Eric Helleiner, it reached maturity only in the past few years, playing a decisive role in the structure and dynamics of the emerging global order.[4]

The financial structure, as pointed out by Susan Strange, is an undeniable source of power. In a market economy, power is in the hands of those who define credit: how it can be created and in what amounts, who can have access to it and under what conditions. At the same time, control of finances eventually also implies control of production. In fact, the consequent economic globalization "results in a very rapid increase in international investment; the predominance of this investment in trade in services; the increasing weight of transnational corporations in international trade and the volume reached by inter-firm trade, and the appearance of extremely concentrated structures of international supply, which lead to global oligopolies resulting from mergers and acquisitions."[5]

Recent technological transformations also are conducive to globalization. The development of telecommunications has reduced the costs of transferring money, restored confidence in the security of international financial transactions, and met the increased demand for international financial services resulting from various factors: the growth of trade, the activities of the multinational corporations, the availability of significant bank deposits following the increase in the international price of petroleum in 1973, the tendency to establish fluctuating exchange rates in the '70s, which contributed to the diversification of international investments in the volatile exchange rate markets, and growing domestic competitive pressures that led financial operators to the international arena.[6]

The development of post-Fordism promises a new and more flexible organization of industrial activity,[7] based on the optimization of the global factors of production (equipment, work, raw materials, stock); on the integration of research, development and marketing networks; and, on reduced costs.[8] Likewise, the development of the post-Fordist production model implies the transnationalization of production, no longer limited to a definite domestic market but flexibly adapted to a diverse global market. It also is conducive to the automation of production and the dissemination of technologies across frontiers, which affect the labor relations established by Fordism within the framework of the welfare state. In fact, it has a significant impact on the bargaining power of the labor force organized in traditional trade unions and favors the coordination of intrafirm labor relations adapted to the new technological conditions and to the requirements of productive restructuring.[9]

Together with financial globalization, the information revolution has proved difficult for governments to control or even, as pointed out scathingly by Roger Williams, to understand. And of course, revolution is not limited to finance but also is conducive to advances in other important fields such as bioengineering, resulting in a dramatic change in the previous technological paradigm.[10]

In short, transformations of the financial structure, the productive structure, and the structure of know-how[11] underlie the process of economic globalization, affecting both the security structure established in the course of the Cold War and furthering a marked increase in trade at the world level. This situation also affected the definition of the role of the state and of civil society.

The Socialization of Globalization: State and Civil Society

Under the pressure of structural transformations in the international economic system, the state is forced to adapt to a new international division of labor, promoting programs of structural adjustment particularly in peripheral countries. This process is, however, contingent upon several factors, including external pressures and demands for internationalization by multinational companies and world financial organizations and the ideological impact of neoliberal ideas, often connected with the demands of domestic technocratic sectors,[12] for structural adjustments toward a market economy. These adjustments in turn generate tensions among various domestic sectors, due especially to the destruction of the welfare state and the social policies associated with it.

As a result, the traditional nation-state is affected both in its external and internal sovereignty. Nevertheless, as Robert Cox pointed out, the state, when acting as an intermediary between the international and the domestic domain, does not lose its autonomy,[13] though it is faced with a more complex web of actors and interests and often is torn between the dynamics of the world market and international politics, on the one hand, and the demands of domestic political and civil society (trade unions, legislatures, political parties, social movements, NGOs, various social networks), on the other.[14]

The many possible responses to these multiple demands give rise to various state forms[15] in terms of greater or lesser internationalization or localization, rather than to a single state form within the context of globalization. States become "agencies of the globalizing world"[16] in their relation to the market,[17] with particular disadvantages for those states that arrive at this process late or find themselves in situations of structural vulnerability and asymmetric interaction with states already adapted to this process.

Equally significant is the birth of civil society and its transnationalization, particularly in the developing societies where the market economy–Western democracy equation is reinforced ideologically. In addition to the current debate on civil society, into the details of which *we* shall not enter in this chapter,[18] I emphasize its globalization. In general terms, analysts agree that the social movements that characterize a global civil society are associated with issues such as civil rights, the environment, gender, minority rights, and so on, and that they form international networks with a growing influence over governments, state policies,[19] nongovernmental organizations, intergovernmental agencies, international organizations, and even transnational companies. In fact, some authors refer to a three-dimensional global dynamic between the state and market, the state and civil society, and the civil society and market, through various transnational and domestic actors. But perhaps the most significant impact of the emerging concept of global civil society, particularly in its liberal-pluralistic version, has been the promotion of democracy at the international level.

Unfortunately, this perspective takes an overly homogeneous view of global civil society and its development. It ignores the fact that global civil society reproduces, at the international level, the conflicts and contradictions of the domestic societies from which it is derived and also generates new conflicts and contradictions.[20] At the domestic level, it often weakens political parties and trade unions, and in the cultural sphere, frequently contributes to greater social fragmentation and increased difficulty in coordinating broader projects and reaching a national consensus. At the international level, the linkage of nongovernmental organizations and social movements of industrialized countries with their counterparts in the developing countries may generate tensions between the financial and ideological power of the former and the development agenda of the latter, especially if the structural sources of inequality are overlooked.

From this point of view, according to James Rosenau, it is evident that we are faced with an international system that is more and more "multi-centric" and no longer only "state-centric,"[21] as in the "realist" perspective, which is becoming increasingly complex. At present, both models seem to coexist, giving rise to various possible future development scenarios for the international economic system.[22]

Along with the multiplication of transnational actors, there also is a multiplication of perceptions with regard to the process of globalization.[23]

Globalization and Regionalization: The Hemispheric Effects

Economic globalization, increasing trade, and commercial interdependence have had a decisive effect on the emergence of economic-political blocs: the European Union (EU), North America (NAFTA), and Southeast Asia linked to Japan. This has generated tension between the predominant tendency toward trade liberalization, regulated to a greater or lesser extent by GATT or the recently created World Trade Organization (WTO), and the increasing orientation toward the formation of regional blocs, with the eventual emergence of new protectionist temptations in the industrialized North.

Nevertheless, globalization and regionalization are not necessarily incompatible. The formation of economic blocs can lead—in the best case, and in the absence of further protectionist measures—on a regional basis toward universalization through the intervention of private actors in various markets, particularly in the realm of finance and international investment.[24] In any case, global productive restructuring is contingent upon financial globalization and the resulting flow of capital and investments, inasmuch as it depends to a large extent on the capacity to finance changes in organization and technology. It follows that the regions with the greatest flow and concentration of investments tend to have the greatest restructuring potential and competitive capacity. Of course, this favors the countries with the highest degree of industrial development, which are most attractive for productive investments.

On the other hand, as Peter Smith points out,[25] the process of regionalization also has a political dimension and requires a political will. The European Union is a good example. In fact, the political and economic domains cannot really be separated, since the dynamics of the national or international market are independent of state action, however minimal. In a way, the market is itself a political mechanism that mediates political conflict, deciding who receives what, when, and how.[26] From this point of view, the state manages pressures in the domestic and international domains through domestic policies and intergovernmental negotiation, which are closely linked. At the same time, the state is becoming a key interlocutor in negotiations, not only with other states but also with firms and corporations, which Strange calls "state-firm" diplomacy. The basic problems of international political economy involve both the transnational market economy and the system of competing states.[27] And the latter, despite the dominant neoliberal discourse, plays a crucial role.

Economic globalization has led to an acceleration of regional and subregional integration in Latin America, with the revitalization of the Andean Pact, CARICOM, and the Central American Economic System (SIECA) and the appearance of new systems aimed at the formation of free trade areas, such as the South American common market (MERCOSUR), the Group of Three, and the Association of Caribbean States. These schemes are aimed at increasing intraregional trade and developing economies of scale, which will lead to greater competitiveness. There also has been a multiplication of bilateral economic complementarity agreements between various Latin American and Caribbean countries.[28] All of these events augur the development in Latin America and the Caribbean of what the Economic Commission for Latin America and the Caribbean (ECLAC) has called "new regionalism" or "open regionalism," meaning a "process of growing economic interdependence at the regional level, promoted both by preferential integration agreements and by other policies within a context of opening and deregulation, in order to increase the competitiveness of the countries of the region."[29]

To a large extent, these initiatives respond to a manifest political will, preceded and encouraged by concerted democratic action among Latin American and Caribbean governments in the 1980s, which resulted in the so-called Rio Group. They also were intended to increase the region's bargaining power with extra-regional actors and, by emphasizing exports, to adapt to the requirements of competitiveness within the international system. In this process, the privatization of state enterprises, deregulation, decentralization, and reform of the state' have gone hand in hand with a restructuring of distributive mechanisms and employment and social policies. The *open regionalism*[30] adopted by Latin America and the Caribbean is a response to the international system's "new rules of the game,"[31] in which older, predominantly intergovernmental agreements are succeeded by a more aggressive entrepreneurial sector and by a new linkage between political elites and entrepreneurs. This new linkage does not always evolve smoothly, since not all of the economic elites support these reforms, particularly in those countries whose development has been highly contingent upon the persistence of a protected market, subsidies, and state support, and on mechanisms of political patronage. Also, political elites sometimes defend the continuity of those mechanisms on the ground of sovereignty or national interests.

These transformations have brought new actors onto the scene. There are many new intergovernmental and nongovernmental organizations, transnational corporations, regional and global organizations, and social networks. New sociopolitical alliances have arisen, and some traditional actors, including political parties and trade unions,[32] have lost influence, partly because of the difficulty of coordinating collective interests in an increasingly complex and diversified sociopolitical environment, partly because of their own inefficiency and corruption, and partly because the new social movements tend to dilute the frontiers of domestic civil society and orient themselves globally.[33] A large literature has arisen on the emergence of new social movements in Latin America and their limitations in the domain of political dynamics.

THE PROCESS OF REGIONALIZATION IN THE CARIBBEAN BASIN

On July 24, 1994, the Association of Caribbean States (ACS) was constituted in Cartagena de Indias, with twenty-five states as full members and twelve as associate members, to encourage the creation of a free trade area among the countries of the region, coordinate their policies vis-à-vis third parties, and facilitate cooperation in other areas.[34] Although the principal promoters of the initiative are the member countries of CARICOM, the ACS responds to a "broader view"[35] of the region as the Caribbean Basin, with overtones of the Third World definition that was fashionable in the '70s, since the members are characterized as developing countries and do not include the United States. The initiative has the support and active participation of the Group of Three (Mexico, Venezuela, and Colombia) and the (more hesitant) backing of the Central American countries,[36] resulting, for the first time, in a system that embraces the region as a whole. Nevertheless, questions arise regarding whether this initiative responds effectively to the aspirations of the Caribbean societies.

Regional Security: The End of the Geopolitical Discourse As An Incentive To Regionalization

Among the results of the end of the Cold War and rise of globalization are the dilution of the Central American crisis, the electoral defeat of the Sandinistas, and the growing isolation of Cuba. Despite the persistence of links with Russia and tensions with the United States, Cuba has become increasingly isolated in the region, and the Cuban model from previous decades has been replaced, among neighboring states and even some leftists in the region, by a kind of condescending solidarity. The threat of a proliferation of socialist regimes in the region has disappeared.

The end of strategic bipolarity has not only reduced the strategic importance of the region and the possibility of alternative sociopolitical systems, but also has reduced the capacity of its political elites to negotiate assistance programs or preferential trade systems (as in the case of the Caribbean Basin Initiative (CBI), the Lomé agreements with the EU, or the Caribbean program with Canada) by accommodating the strategic interests of the Western bloc. Use of the "Cuban card"[37] to press for assistance has become more difficult. The new regional security agenda assigns priority to matters like control of drug traffic and migration, the environment, and the consolidation of democracy,[38] of relatively secondary strategic importance compared to the importance previously attached to Cuban-Soviet influence.

This agenda also is influenced more often by domestic politics, particularly in the United States as shown by the intervention in Haiti, significantly conditioned by public concern over illegal immigration, accusations of racism by the congressional "black caucus," and the promotion of democracy in the hemisphere, to the point of backing the restoration of a government which, although elected democratically and with strong support from the people, in other days would have been considered by the U. S. government "radical" and probably "pro-communist." Similar comments can be made with regard to the persistence of hostility toward Cuba, motivated partly by the domestic political weight of Cuban-American organizations and by the fear of an avalanche of immigrants. In short, the possibilities of local political elites continuing to obtain external assistance by means of the systems established during the Cold War have disappeared or diminished considerably.

In fact, the definition of a regional security agenda is difficult, not only because of the growing domestic pressures of actors with different capacities and political power but also because of the difficulty of determining, once the Communist threat has disappeared, what threat remains that might justify the establishment of a collective security regime in the Caribbean Basin.[39] The ACS, for example, does not provide for cooperation in matters of regional collective security.[40] Concerns about regional security have shifted from strategic-military issues to police and intelligence matters. Despite the persistence of border disputes between the various countries in the region, including some maritime demarcations, there is not much interest in regional security agreements or measures of mutual confidence.[41]

On the other hand, as Anthony Maingot points out in his recent book, the concerns of regional governments (and to a large extent those of the United States) are shifting more and more to problems arising from the internationalization of corruption and violence, through the frequent relations of bureaucratic and financial sectors with drug traffic or organized crime networks or with terrorist groups and organizations.[42] Various forms of international cooperation related to these problems have arisen, as have transnational networks of an illegal or criminal nature that eventually may affect the political stability of countries in the region.

In sum, discussion of the geostrategic importance of the Caribbean Basin has been succeeded by a more pragmatic discourse geared predominantly to economic issues and framed by neoliberal ideas and international economic pressures.

From Geopolitical to Geoeconomic Discourse

The structural transformations outlined earlier have had a variety of effects on the economies and societies of the Caribbean Basin, but we can identify some general trends.[43] Generally speaking, in reaction to the debt crisis in the '80s and other international pressures, most of the countries in the region chose new development strategies. These strategies replaced the policy of import substitution (i.e., active intervention by the state to protect domestic markets and promote specific economic policies) with export promotion, diversification, and the consequent objective of increasing competitiveness in the international economy. These programs sought to reduce the role of the state in the economy and to encourage privatization and productive investments.[44]

The Caribbean economies have been characterized mainly by the exploitation of natural resources, agricultural production, the production of semimanufactured goods of low value-added, limited diversification, and the so-called "Dutch disease."[45] Structural readjustment meant a reduction and redefinition of the traditional functions of the state, based traditionally on clientelism, political patronage, and populistic agreements,[46] through the reduction of public expenditure, privatization, deregulation, and eventual (not always fully achieved) economic opening and liberalization, along with the promotion of macroeconomic policies (fiscal and monetary) in keeping with the need to project an image of reform and economic stability and an attractive climate for foreign capital and technology.

This process had several implications. To attract foreign investment, the state needed to improve fiscal conditions, infrastructure, training, and labor relations (e.g., in the export processing zones of the Dominican Republic, Jamaica, and Puerto Rico). The state must become an effective interlocutor with the potential foreign investors. The state also has to create the necessary conditions for the development of the local private sector, channeling domestic production into internationally competitive exports. Finally, the state must dilute the existing social contract, including redistributive, welfare, and labor policy, with significant social and political costs.

And in fact, despite the positive effects of the export-processing zones in terms of economic growth, they have mainly given rise to assembly industries, with limited skilled labor requirements (hence the recruitment of female workers and the consequent gender imbalances). In an environment of global productive restructuring, with increasing requirements in regard to high technology and skilled labor and with world trade focused increasingly on trade in manufactures of high value-added and services, this is hardly optional.

Furthermore, regionalism sometimes served as an alternative to the development of economies of scale, broader markets and the growth of foreign trade, as regions looked inward to avoid exclusion from the international economic system in case of protectionist policies by the industrialized nations. For the small countries of the Caribbean Basin, particularly the non-Spanish-speaking Caribbean islands, these anxieties become all the more pressing in view of the possible disappearance of such preferential agreements as the Caribbean Basin Initiative with the United States, Lomé with the European Union, and CARIBCAN with Canada, and of Mexico's eventual competitive advantage from its incorporation into NAFTA. In view of the limited domestic and subregional market and the consequent lack of attractiveness for foreign investments, these countries looked to free trade and economic complementarity agreements. Similar concerns led to the creation of the Group of Three by Mexico, Colombia, and Venezuela (despite their different priorities, which I have analyzed elsewhere). Free trade agreements led to the encouragement of active participation by the entrepreneurial sector. They also implied a significant cession of sovereignty, particularly in view of the need for the harmonization of macroeconomic policies and coordination of foreign policies (particularly in trade).

The Sociopolitical Impacts of Globalization and Regionalization

The rescaling and internationalization of the state in the Caribbean Basin had significant political and social consequences, most notably the end of the social and political contract based on the distributive capacity of the state involving policies that favored various sectors through the resources obtained within the framework of external assistance and the placing of some products in preferential markets. In principle, this picture can be extended to the non-Spanish-speaking Caribbean islands and to Cuba, though not to the Central American countries,[47] and was reflected to a certain extent in the populist policies of the Institutional Revolutionary Party (PRI) in Mexico and the Venezuelan government (though not in the case of Colombia).

Given this general trend toward redistributive mechanisms rooted in clientelistic and populist political systems, the external debt crisis and the subsequent adjustment programs clearly implied a reorientation of state policies. One should differentiate, however, in the domestic entrepreneurial sector, generally developed with protectionist policies and state subsidies,[48] between those sectors capable of adapting to international competition and others more rooted in the domestic market and more hesitant with regard to the opening. The state was obliged to negotiate with multinational companies (to attract capital and technology), international financial organizations (to renegotiate the external debt and obtain additional credits), and other governments (to establish free trade and economic cooperation agreements). In this process, links between traditional political elites and emerging technocratic sectors have been decisive, since the latter have contributed not only the necessary know-how for adjustment and trade liberalization but also the necessary legitimation vis-à-vis the international interlocutors.

Under the pressure of external demands and the need for rapid and efficient economic reform, neoliberal policies in the 1980s often regulated the demands and expectations of the population to second place, giving rise to political and social tensions and considerable difficulty in reaching a consensus regarding the new development strategies. At the same time, the speed and efficiency required by the international environment for these programs make it difficult to formulate medium- and short-term policies capable of compensating for these difficulties or to implement industrial and research policies whereby it will be possible, in the long term, to compete more advantageously in the international market.

Consequently, the adjustment programs implied, in their first stage, a significant expansion of the range of loser groups and sectors in the Caribbean societies. The new economic policies have affected a large part of the rural population (with the elimination of subsidies and the decline in the international prices of agricultural products),[49] public administration and civil service workers, state enterprises, the trade union movement in general, and the female unskilled labor force in particular (with the incorporation of the new production nuclei as low-cost manpower and with limited labor rights). At the same time, there has been a worsening of poverty among the low-income population, in general, due to the elimination of redistributive social policies and to increased unemployment and underemployment.

The most evident sociopolitical costs of this general process are the weakening of support for the traditional political parties (now incapable of providing the benefits rooted in the former system of political patronage and clientelism and increasingly identified with corruption scandals), the aforementioned collapse of the trade unions (often cornerstones in the original formation of some political parties),[50] and the proliferation of social movements in the face of the incapacity of the political organizations to coordinate sectoral interests. As I have described elsewhere,[51] throughout the Caribbean there has been a significant development of grassroots and community organizations, groups and associations of women, religious organizations, environmentalist movements, and human rights organizations, which have had a significant impact on the emergence of civil society, on governmental organizations and agencies, and on the channels of institutionalized political expression such as the political parties, trade unions, and legislatures.

In short, the social and political contracts that underwrote the democratic systems in the region underwent a radical redefinition, with considerable impact on the legitimacy of the systems and their governability. Particularly in their first stages, the adjustment programs implied a sociopolitical and socioeconomic vicious circle that few political elites managed to foresee or break beforehand. The best examples are perhaps the successive crises in Venezuela and the 1994–95 financial crisis in Mexico (preceded by the Chiapas rebellion and the assassination of the presidential candidate Colosio), but similar developments can be glimpsed in the rest of the Caribbean Basin. The resulting conflicts have had a significant effect on the state's capacity to govern in democratic political cultures, from the Westminster parliamentary model adopted in the English-speaking Caribbean to the single-party, two-party, or many-party presidential variants established in Latin America.

THE ASSOCIATION OF CARIBBEAN STATES: REGIONALIZATION AND "DEMOCRATIC DEFICIT"

As we have seen, the response of the political and governmental elites to the challenges imposed by globalization has involved not only internal economic restructuring but also efforts to expand the subregional economic arena by means of free trade agreements. The reactivation of the

Central American Common Market (CACM), following the process of regional pacification that took place after the signing of the Esquipulas Agreement, and the efforts of the Contadora Group and CARICOM, have been linked to the creation of the Group of Three (G-3) in 1989. These three systems, along with intersystem and bilateral agreements with Cuba and the Dominican Republic, paved the way for the constitution of the ACS in July 1994.

The ACS is an "organization of consultation, cooperation and concerted action,"[52] the basic aim of which is to promote a free trade system in the Caribbean Basin and to increase intraregional trade and cooperation.[53] One of the main points of reference in this process of regionalization is the establishment of NAFTA and the launching of the Enterprise for the Americas Initiative (EAI) by President Bush in 1990.[54]

I have analyzed formerly[55] the different expectations of the various components of the ACS with regard to NAFTA. Briefly, while for the Central American countries and the Caribbean islands the establishment of NAFTA could eventually mean the elimination of the nonreciprocal benefits of preferential trade contemplated by the CBI, as well as competition from Mexico for access to the North American market,[56] the members of the ACS generally view Mexico as a potential bridge for linkage to NAFTA. The inclusion of Cuba, however, does not help make the ACS a particularly attractive interlocutor for the United States, in the present circumstances at least. On the other hand, the asymmetry of economic potentials, the diversity of priorities and objectives, and the different individual or subregional bargaining power of each of the countries in the ACS are not conducive to easy agreement. In fact, although there have been rapprochements and attempts at economic linkage between the Central American countries and the members of CARICOM, the former have clearly tended to develop their own independent strategy in their links both with NAFTA and with Mexico, even after signing onto the ACS. At the same time, the political crisis that led to the impeachment of President Carlos Andrés Pérez in Venezuela, with the subsequent interruption of some of the economic reforms launched by his government and the country's persisting financial crisis, have not only hampered Venezuela in continuing a regional policy toward the Caribbean but also have given rise to difficulties in relations with Colombia, its principal trade partner after the United States—difficulties aggravated by the recrudescence of border tensions, particularly as a result of the activities of Colombian guerrillas. Last, the membership of Mexico in the system is seriously threatened by the effects of the crisis of December 1994, with its evident repercussions for Mexico's ability to coordinate multilateral relations with NAFTA and the United States (if there ever was an effective possibility of that).

To this situation the uncertainties of U. S. domestic policy are added: the vague attitude of the Clinton administration prior to the Miami summit; the absence of a definite schedule for the creation of a hemispheric free trade area by the year 2005; and the changes that may eventually take place for the promotion of this U. S. initiative as a result of the control acquired by the Republican members of Congress. Perhaps the best example of these difficulties is President Clinton's decision to assign $20 billion for assistance to Mexico through the executive branch of government, evading the probable refusal of the $40 billion he originally requested from Congress. Hopes tend to focus more and more on the South American countries, particularly on the eventual appearance of a South American Free Trade Area (SAFTA), based on MERCOSUR and the Latin American Integration Association (ALADI) (in which the Caribbean islands and the Central American countries do not participate). This development is being promoted by the new Brazilian administration as part of a reorientation of that country's hemispheric policy regarding MERCOSUR, including increasing links with Venezuela and the Andean Pact. The growth in intraregional trade since 1991, sometimes suggested as an alternative strategy in case of eventual exclusion from other regional blocs, and the political concerted action developed in the Rio Group, both tend to exclude the interests of the small Caribbean and Central American countries. Tensions have arisen, too, over the location and personnel of the ACS General Secretariat, motivated by domestic political circumstances in the member countries.[57]

In a recent paper, Henry Gill points out six problems the ACS must address. First, the definition of an exclusive space that does not overlap with other regional and subregional organizations or integration schemes and, in particular, one that differs from NAFTA in taking the Caribbean area seriously. Second, the definition of specific objectives, particularly in the field of investment and trade, and the coordination of the efforts of the various schemes regarding the interests of the ACS. Third, defining the participation and interaction of the regional actors, bearing in mind the central role assumed by CARICOM and the question of states and territories associated with extra-regional actors (e.g., the French Overseas Departments, the U. S. Virgin Islands, and Puerto Rico). Fourth, specifying an adequate budget, given the present economic difficulties in the region. Fifth, defining the degree of effective commitment to the ACS of the full and associate members who signed and eventually ratified the constitutive Convention of July 24, 1994. And sixth, defining the role of the private sector, in principle a "social actor" like all other sectors, without institutionalized participation. As Gill points out, many substantial problems still remain regarding the ACS's objectives, purview, and membership,[58] in addition to the vagueness and lack of definition of the institutional mechanisms and their consolidation.

Most of these observations were partially confirmed at the ACS summit in Port-of-Spain in August 1995.

I have analyzed formerly the increasing linkage and interdependence of basic movements, religious and cultural groups, women's and environmentalists' organizations, human rights movements, and academic networks in the region and how they have attempted to offer criticisms and alternatives to the projects promoted by dominant elites.[59] Nevertheless, the ACS docs not contemplate a recognition of these "social actors," beyond a general reference in its constitutive Convention, which leaves the matter largely to the discretion of the Council of Ministers.[60]

In fact, according to the recommendations of the West Indian Commission (WIC), the ACS could contemplate, in principle, the establishment of a regional Assembly or Parliament[61] on the model of the European Union, with objectives transcending the establishment of a free trade area. But although the Parliament can partly lessen the "democratic deficit" arising in the process of regionalization, it limits political representation to the political parties, with no provision for the other organizations and movements in civil society.

Paradoxically, despite the reactivation of networks among the political parties of the region (at least the Christian Democrats and Social Democrats),[62] there is no significant public debate about integration, regional identity, or democratic participation.

As I have mentioned, this process generates a marked difference in the regional identifications assumed by the various social and political movements and organizations, as well as their growing differentiation from the political organizations that coordinate traditional interests, such as the political parties and traditional trade unions, the former weakened by the reduction of the state's distributive capacity, with its accompanying systems of political patronage and clientelism, the latter by the economic restructuring. The deterioration of the traditional political organizations, such as the parties (affected not only by the shrinking of the state but also by growing public awareness of corruption),[63] has led to the appearance of social movements and organizations expressing the interests of cultural, gender, ethnic, and religious groups lacking political representation. The lack of institutional channels of political representation by these movements and organizations, besides promoting a "transnationalized civil society" or a regional "social community,"[64] can also result in a social and political fragmentation that can, however, enrich democracy and pluralism provided it takes place within a framework of participatory decision making and shared values and interests. At the same time, if taken to an extreme, it can lead to the emergence of various forms of fundamentalism, currently more ethnic- or gender-based than ideological.

REGIONALIZATION, SOVEREIGNTY, AND IDENTITY
IN THE CARIBBEAN BASIN

This general view of the impact of global, regional, and national transformations in the Caribbean Basin raises again questions about its existence as an explicitly differentiated region. Some analysts ask why the region is so divided and not further advanced in its integration.[65] Others question its viability as a "functional" and "coherent" region that can benefit from integration beyond the common interest in trade and regional security. Some authors limit these questions to a view of the region confined to the English-speaking or island Caribbean; others assign it some immanent identifying property or distinctive regional essence.

What I would stress is the fact that in recent years a social imagery has made its appearance, with a central point of reference: the debate regarding regionalism and regional integration. In this debate, regionalism consists basically of a response to external and domestic challenges that call forth a collective response, the "construction of a regional community."[66] This process implies the identification of common values and purposes and regional identity.[67] This identity can be articulated in three aspects.

The first is the extent to which the societies have a common historical experience and are faced with common problems. In the case of the Caribbean Basin, this common historical experience is related to its genealogy as a geopolitical unit, reinforced by various perceptions—ethnohistorical, economic, political—of its unity.[68]

The second derives from the sociocultural, political, and/or economic links that distinguish it from the rest of the world. In this respect, despite the cultural, linguistic, and political barriers dividing it, the Caribbean Basin has promoted various forms of cooperation among the states by means of formal and multilateral mechanisms, such as the OAS or SELA, and the free trade and economic cooperation agreements promoted in the past few years.[69]

Third and lastly, there is the extent to which they have developed various organizations to deal with collective matters. The creation of the Association of Caribbean States is an example, even though it is not at present "a consolidated political actor." Nevertheless, regionalism implies the need to go further in the construction of a regional community by furthering integration. This process transcends intergovernmental initiatives and is aimed at the construction of a "social community" of a regional nature, not only through the consolidation of a regional interstate collective actor but also by developing mechanisms of participation by civil society in regional decision making and by developing a common collective imagery of an inclusive, not exclusive, regional identity. This is the long-term objective of regional integration in terms of the construction of a community of shared values, common objectives, and regional identity.[70]

In this process of formation, there is one common triggering factor: the need to cope collectively with the global transformations facing the region, since individual options are increasingly limited in a globalizing world. Nevertheless, in addition to the difficulties discussed in the previous pages, there are still others worthy of note, however briefly. I shall mention them in order to suggest some fundamental items of a regional sociopolitical agenda.

In the first place, the coordination of collective responses implies the erosion of national sovereignty. Although this is a process that is taking place everywhere due to the reduction of the autonomy of the states in the face of economic globalization, in the Caribbean Basin it touches very sensitive fibers. One reason is that the consolidation of the nation-state grew out of various states' claims for post-colonial self-determination. As Hilbourne Watson points out, in the case of the Caribbean islands,[71] the articulation of national sovereignty in the region was delayed and took place within the context of its integration into the international system of states. Hence, the very mention of a cession of sovereignty in terms of its gradual and partial "regionalization"[72] gives rise to hesitation.

In the second place, there is the difficulty of overcoming the "democratic deficit" that all integration entails, which, as I pointed out, is particularly evident in the regionalization of the Caribbean Basin in terms of the principle, "We will decide for you, and in your interests, but without you." There is a clear example of this difficulty in the case of the European Union, the system that has advanced furthest toward the constitution of a "social community" and the coordination of institutionalized mechanisms of political participation. Even so, this deficit is particularly evident in the role of the European Parliament and in the absence of mechanisms of participation by civil society in the EU.[73]

In the third place, the process of integration, to be successful, must lead to the creation of adequate legal institutions for more active public participation in decision making related to regionalization, its stages and advances, and the interests to which it responds. This is especially important in order to avoid fundamentalist responses to the erosion of national sovereignty, as well as the emergence of "globalist" temptations[74] on the part of bureaucratic sectors. In this regard, the development of democratic and pluralist institutional mechanisms is imperative in bringing the process of regionalization to a successful confusion.

NOTES

1. Richard Stubbs and Geoffrey R. D. Underhill (eds.), *Political Economy and the Changing Global Order*, (London: MacMillan, 1994), 554 pages; Stephen Gill and David Law, *The Global Political Economy: Perspectives, Problems and Policies*, (Baltimore: Johns Hopkins University Press, 1988); Robert Gilpin, *The Political Economy of International Relations*, (Princeton, N. J.: Princeton University Press, 1987).

2. Carlos Moneta and Carlos Quenan (eds.), *Las reglas de juego. América Latina, globalización y regionalismo* (Buenos Aires: Corrector, 1994), 191 pages; Mitchell Bernard, "Post-Fordism, Transnational Production, and the Changing Global Political Economy," in R. Stubbs and G. R. D. Underhill (eds.), (London: MacMillan, 1994), 216–29.

3. Carlos Moneta, "El proceso de globalización: percepciones y desarrollos," in Carlos Moneta and Carlos Quenan (eds.), (Buenos Aires: Corrector, 1994), 147–65.

4. Eric Helleiner, "From Bretton Woods to Global Finance: A World Turned Upside Down," in R. Stubbs and G. R. D. Underhill (eds.), (London: MacMillan, 1994), 167–73. He adds that this process not only implied the dilution of the ideas of Keynes and White regarding the protection of the social welfare state, but also favored the preservation of the autonomy of the United States' policies vis-à-vis its increasing external and internal deficits, reinforcing its supremacy in the new global financial system.

5. Moneta and Quenan, 1994, 15.

6. Helleiner, 165–6.

7. Bernard, 1994, 216–17.

8. Moneta and Quenan, 1994, 11.

9. In fact, it implies the destruction of the trade unions as political forces and their replacement by "pro-management company-based labor unions that acted as an unofficial administrative arm of management," (Bernard, 1994, 219).

10. Hilbourne Watson, "Introduction: The Caribbean and the Techno-Paradigm Shift in Global Capitalism," in Hilbourne Watson (ed.), (Boulder: Lynne Rienner, 1994), 1–8.

11. We follow Strange in this classification. Susan Strange, *States and Markets* (London: Pinter Publ., 1988), 266 pages; and Susan Strange, "Global government and global opposition," in G. Parry (ed.), (Cambridge: Edward Elgar, 1994), 20–33.

12. Thomas Bierstecker, "The "Triumph of Neoclassical Economics in the Developing World: Policy Convergence and Bases of Governance in

the International Economic Order," in J. Rosenau and E. O. Czempiel (eds.), (Cambridge: Cambridge University Press, 1992), 115–27.

13. Robert Cox, *Production, Power, and World Order: Social Forces in the Making of History*, (New York: Columbia University Press, 1987), 399–400.

14. Richard Stubbs and G. R. D. Underhill, "State Policies and Global Changes," in R. Stubbs and G. R. D. Underhill (eds.), (London: MacMillan, 1994), 423.

15. Robert Cox, "Towards a Post-Hegemonic Conceptualization of World Order: Reflections on the Relevancy of Ibn Khaldun," in J. Rosenau and E. O. Czempiel (eds.), (Cambridge: Cambridge University Press, 1992), 143.

16. Cox, 1992, 145.

17. Samir Amin goes further, arguing that these processes entail two new elements: "the deterioration of the centralized nation-state and the subsequent disappearance of the link between the sphere of reproduction and accumulation and that of political and social control, which up until now had been determined precisely by the frontiers of that centralized nation-state; and the caducity of the contrast between centralized industrial regions and nonindustrialized peripheral regions, and the appearance of new aspects of polarization," Samir Amin, "El futuro de la polarización global," in *Nueva Sociedad*, no. 132 (1994), 120.

18. In this respect, Jean Cohen and Andrew Amato, *Civil Society and Political Theory* (Cambridge: MIT Press, 1992), 772 pages; and for a more recent critical review from the Marxist or post-Marxist points of view, Carlos Vilas, "La hora de la sociedad civil," in *Análisis Político* (Bogotá), no. 21 (January–April 1994), 5–13; and Laura Macdonald, "Globalizing Civil Society: Interpreting International NGOs in Central America," in *Millenium*, (vol. 23, no. 2), (London: Summer 1994), 267–85. As an operative definition of the concept, we take that provided by Diamond: "the realm of organized social life that is voluntary, self-generating, [largely] self-supporting, autonomous from the state, and bound by a legal order or set of shared values [which] involves citizens acting collectively in a public sphere," Larry Diamond, "Toward Democratic Consolidation. Rethinking Civil Society," in *Journal of Democracy*, (1994), 5.

19. Margaret Keck and Kathryn Sikkink, "Transnational Issue Networks in International Politics," Ms., (1994), 7–20.

20. Laura Macdonald, "Globalizing Civil Society: Interpreting International NGOs in Central America," in *Millenium*, vol. 23, no. 2, (London: summer 1994), 285.

21. James Rosenau, "Citizenship in a Changing Global Order," in James Rosenau and E. O. Czempiel (eds.), 1992.

22. SELA, *Scenarios of World Change*, XIX Regular Meeting of the Latin American Council, Caracas, (25 to 29 October 1993), SP/CL/XIX.0/DT, no. 13, 86–90.

23. SELA, *Report of the Meeting of Experts for the Analysis of Long-term Scenarios*, XX Regular Meeting of the Latin American Council, Mexico, (30 May to 3 June 1994), SP/CL/XX.0/Di, no. 9, 5.

24. Moneta and Quenan, 1994, 16.

25. Peter Smith, *The Challenge of Integration: Europe and the Americas* (New Brunswick: Transaction Publishers, 1993), 5.

26. Geoffrey Underhill "Conceptualizing the changing global order," in R. Stubbs and G. Underhill (eds.), (London: MacMillan, 1994), 18–19.

27. Underhill, 1994, 21.

28. As pointed out in a recent ECLAC document, "The new generation of agreements show marked differences from those entered into in the past decade. They are usually aimed at the establishment of free trade for almost all trade within a short time, and they usually add interesting linking elements as regards infrastructural interconnection, facilitation and promotion of mutual investments and exchange of services, and expeditious mechanisms for the settlement of disputes, among others. These agreements usually unite countries having similar orientations as regards their trade and economic policies, or other neighboring countries, in which there are already important economic links" (ECLAC, *Desarrollo reciente de los procesos de integración en América Latina y el Caribe*, LC/R.1381, (5 May 1994), 5). At the time of the drafting of the document, ECLAC identified the existence of twenty-six economic complementarity agreements of this kind.

29. ECLAC, *El regionalismo abierto en América Latina y el Caribe*, LC/L.808 (CEG.19/3), (13 January 1994), 2. The open regionalism deployed in the region is likewise viewed as a hedge against the possibility of increased protectionist measures on the part of the industrialized countries and constitutes an "important function, in this case a defense mechanism against the effects of eventual protectionist pressures in extra-regional markets" (ibid., 2).

30. ECLAC, LC/L.808, 13 January 1993.

31. Moneta and Quenan, 1994, reference in the title of the book.

32. David Smith, "Central American and Caribbean People: Challenges and Needs During the 1990s," paper presented at the IV Conference of the Association of Caribbean Economists (Curaçao, 22–25 June 1993) on trade unions/waterman.

33. Amato and Cohen, Keck and Sikkink, Diamond, Macdonald.

34. Association of Caribbean States, *Convention Establishing the Association of Caribbean States* (Cartagena de Indias, 24 July 1994).

35. The "broader view" responds both to the suggestions of the Bourne Report to the CARICOM meeting of 1989 and to those of the West Indian Commission of 1992. Andrés Serbin, "¿Una reconfiguración de la Cuenca del Caribe?" in *Nueva Sociedad* (Caracas), no. 133 (September–October 1994), 20–26.

36. Ibid.

37. Anthony Maingot, "Cuba and the Commonwealth Caribbean: Playing the Cuban Card," in Barry Levine (ed.), *The New Cuban Presence in the Caribbean* (Boulder: Westview, 1983).

38. CLADDE-FLACSO, *El Caribe en la Postguerra Fría* (Santiago: CLADDE-FLACSO, 1994), 351 pages; and Andrés Serbin (ed.), *La nueva agenda de seguridad en el Caribe*, in Cuadernos del INVESP, no. 2 (July–December 1993), 96 pages.

39. In this respect, Serbin, 1993; Anthony Maingot, *The United States and the Caribbean* (Boulder: Westview, 1994), 260 pages, and CLADDE-FLACSO, 1994.

40. Convention establishing the Association of Caribbean States, 1994.

41. Serbin, 1993.

42. Maingot, *The United States and the Caribbean*, particularly chaps. 7 and 8.

43. In this respect, ECLAC and SELA documents quoted, and in the specific case of the Caribbean islands, with special reference to the members of CARICOM, Stephen Quick, "The International Economy and the Caribbean: The 1990s and Beyond," in Jorge Domínguez, Robert Pastor, and Delisle Worrell (eds.), *Democracy in the Caribbean* (Baltimore: Johns Hopkins University Press, 1993), 212–28, and Hilbourne Watson (ed.), *The Caribbean in the Global Political Economy* (Boulder: Lynne Rienner, 1994).

44. Basically, structural adjustment implies a reduction and redefinition of the state's economic intervention in the economy, along with increased emphasis on the market for the allocation of scarce goods and resources (Bierstecker, 1992, 108).

45. Quick defines the "Dutch disease" as the situation in which "a very small country finds a ready world market for one product, the export boom in that product pulls local resources away from other industries and undermines their competitiveness" (Quick, 1993, 216). Despite the reference to small countries, the same definition applies to Venezuela.

46. Anthony Payne, "Westminster Adapted: The Political Order of the Commonwealth Caribbean," in Jorge Domínguez *et al.* (eds.), (Baltimore: Johns Hopkins University Press, 1993), 57–73.

47. Evelyne Huber, "The Future of Democracy in the Caribbean," in Jorge Domínguez *et al.* (eds.), (Baltimore: Johns Hopkins University Press, 1993), 74–96.

48. Watson refers specifically to the fact that in the English-speaking Caribbean there is only a mercantilist entrepreneurial sector, incapable of adapting to international competition and economic growth (Hilbourne Watson, "State / Nation-State, Neo-Liberalism and Restructuring: Global Issues in Caribbean Reality," paper presented at the International Studies Association Conference, Washington, D. C. (March 28–April 1, 1994), 15–16). Quick (1993) also refers to the limitations of the Caribbean entrepreneurs.

49. Kai-Alexander Kaiser, *North America and the Caribbean Basin: Viable Paths to a Greater North American Market*, North American Forum Working Paper No. 94/1, Conference Report (January 14–16, 1994), Wattis Room, Littlefield Center, Stanford University.

50. Huber, 1993.

51. Andrés Serbin, "Transnational Relations and Regionalism in the Caribbean," in *ANNALS* (AAPSS), no. 533, (May 1994), 139–50; and Andrés Serbin, "Integración y relaciones transnacionales: el entramado social del proceso de regionalización en la Cuenca del Caribe," in *Perfiles Latinoamericanos* (FLASCO-México), Year 3, No. 4, (June 1994), 7–36.

52. Convention establishing the ACS, 1994, 6.

53. Serbin, "Una reconfiguración de la Cuenca del Caribe."

54. Preparatory documentation of the ACS; Association of Caribbean States, *Documentos preparatorios de la Reunión de Caracas* (29 June 1994).

55. Serbin, "Una reconfiguración de la Cuenca del Caribe."

56. Henry Gill, "The NAFTA Problematique and the Challenges for the Caribbean Community," paper presented at the Conference on "The Caribbean: Range of Choice for the 90's," North-South Center, Miami (10–11 September 1993), 33 pages; and David Lewis, "Los acuerdos regionales de libre comercio y el Caribe: retos y oportunidades del Tratado de Libre Comercio Norteamericano," in Andrés Serbin and Joseph Tulchin (eds.), (1994), 115–70.

57. In an August 1995 summit in Port-of-Spain, the ACS was formally launched, the Venezuelan diplomat Simón Molina Duarte was elected as Secretary-General, and the headquarters of the ACS were in Port-of-Spain. The conference focused on trade, tourism, and transport.

58. Henry Gill, 1995, 15.

59. Serbin, "Transnational Relations and Regionalism in the Caribbean," and "Integración y relaciones transnacionales."

60. In this respect, it is to be noted that in the English version of the Convention establishing the ACS, reference is made to "social partners," and in the Spanish version, "actores sociales," which would include, indistinctly we presume, entrepreneurial organizations, political parties, and social movements.

61. West Indian Commission, *Time for Action* (Bridgeport: WIC, 1992).

62. In September 1994, the Christian Democratic Organization of America (ODCA) met in Aruba to discuss the subject of "The Caribbean vis-à-vis the year 2000," and more recently the Socialist International reactivated its regional presence with a meeting held in Haiti in January 1995.

63. Maingot, *The United States and the Caribbean.*

64. Serbin, "Una reconfiguración de la Cuenca del Caribe."

65. Jorge Domínguez, Robert Pastor, and Delisle Worrell (eds.), *Democracy in the Caribbean* (Baltimore: Johns Hopkins University Press, 1993), 11.

66. Van R. Whiting, "The Dynamics of Regionalization: Road Map to the Open Future?", in Peter Smith (ed.), (New Brunswick: Transaction Publishers, 1993), 42; Manfred Mols, "The Integration Agenda: A Framework for Comparison," in Peter Smith (ed.), (New Brunswick: Transaction Publishers, 1993), 51.

67. Whiting, 1993, 18.

68. Whiting, 1993, 19.

69. Anthony Bryan and Andres Serbin (eds.), *Distant Cousins: The Caribbean-Latin American Relations* (North-South Center, University of Miami: Transaction Press, 1996).

70. Anthony Maingot, "A Region Becoming: Historical Conjuncture and Ideology in the Shaping of Caribbean Politics," paper presented at the ODCA Conference on "El Caribe frente al Siglo XXI," Aruba (9–10 September 1994), 5–19.

71. Watson, "State/Nation-State, Neo-Liberalism and Restructuring," 5.

72. Whiting, 1993, 3.

73. Karlheinz Neureither, "The syndrome of democratic deficit in the European Community," in G. Parry (ed.), (Cambridge: Edward Elgar, 1994), 94–110; and, John Pinder, "Interdependence, democracy and federalism," in G. Parry (ed.), (Cambridge: Edward Elgar, 1994), 111–25, with respect to the democratic deficit in the EU.

74. Michel Rogalski, "El auge de la fractura Norte-Sur. ¿Es posible un gobierno global?", in *Nueva Sociedad*, no. 132, (July–August 1994), 100–17.

5

THE POWERS, THE PIRATES, AND INTERNATIONAL NORMS AND INSTITUTIONS IN THE AMERICAN MEDITERRANEAN

JORGE I. DOMÍNGUEZ

The international relations of the American Mediterranean have never been limited just to relations among states. Since the sixteenth century, the powers and the pirates have helped shape the international environment of the lands and peoples around the contours of the Caribbean Sea and the Gulf of Mexico. In so doing, they have interacted with each other and with "local" actors in and around the American Mediterranean. These local actors have been quite varied as well, ranging from states to individuals. The issues over which there has been contestation cover the agenda of international relations, including power and territory, wealth and status, and individual hopes and fears.

The region's international relations have featured both a "formal sector," namely, relations among states, as well as an "informal sector," namely, relations among non-state actors and relations between them and the states active in the region. These non-state actors have had at times both economic and military resources. In part because of the presence of such non-state actors and in part because the American Mediterranean has characteristically been under the hegemonic influence of a major power that has sought to shape the conduct of international actors, the American Mediterranean has long been a laboratory for the formulation and implementation of norms and rules of "proper" conduct in international affairs: major powers have sought to outlaw piracy, forbid the slave trade and, more recently, foster democracy and markets. Although there has been an extraordinary change in the details of both structure and norms, some structural and normative features in the region's international relations have been remarkably resilient.[1]

Today, as in the past, the peoples of the region are not left to their own joys and miseries. At least one major power, now the United States, claims a right to shape the international and, to some degree, the domestic circumstances of the region. Now, as in the past, important territorial disputes remain unsettled between several of the states in the region. Such disputes have brought states in the recent past to the edge of military conflict. In the late 1980s, for example, the boundary dispute between Venezuela and Colombia brought their navies to the edge of shooting; one reason cited by Venezuelan military officers who sought to overthrow the government twice in 1992 was their perception that the civilians in government were "selling out" the homeland.

Today, as previously, non-state actors have substantial military power and can credibly threaten some existing governments. For many years, insurgents and drug traffickers have fought against the Colombian government; for the most part, such non-state actors remain powerful and still in the field. They use their substantial military power directly in cross-border activities to advance their pecuniary ends. Yesterday's pirates are the ancestors of today's international drug traffickers.

But the present is not just like the past. The countries touched by the waters of the Caribbean Sea in the 1990s belong to an international subsystem whose structure has changed and whose norms are evolving. This chapter explores the observable continuities in order to highlight what has changed since the end of the Cold War in Europe. Although there will be some reference to various countries in the American Mediterranean, the main focus of this work is on the Caribbean Islands and, to a lesser degree, Venezuela.

THE STRUCTURE OF THE CARIBBEAN'S INTERNATIONAL SUBSYSTEM: STATES

Military Hegemony

From the late fifteenth century, a single great power has ordinarily had military command of the Caribbean—first Spain, then England, and, in the twentieth century, the United States have been the region's preeminent military powers. Such military preeminence had always been contested by one or more major powers. England contested Spanish power in the Caribbean in the sixteenth century. France contested England's power until the Napoleonic Wars. England and the United States were rivals in the nineteenth century. In the twentieth century, Germany and, later, the Soviet Union, contested U. S. power.[2]

Thus we come to the first dramatic transformation of the structure of the international system as it affects the Caribbean. For the first time since the sixteenth century, only one major power has impressive and uncontested military clout in the American Mediterranean. The collapse of the Soviet Union and the end of the Cold War in Europe have led to the end of military contestation of U. S. power in the American Mediterranean by an extracontinental power. There is no military alliance between Cuba and the Russian Federation, even if there remains some collaboration in intelligence gathering (especially for commercial purposes) between their two governments.

POLITICAL AND ECONOMIC POLYCENTRICITY

Beyond the military level, however, the Caribbean's international subsystem remains vibrantly polycentric. A great many countries external to the region—not just the United States—have had and retain substantial interests and active engagement in the Caribbean. France, the United Kingdom, and the Netherlands possess territories in the Caribbean; though most of these lands are self-governing, sovereign authority (and often considerable budget support) remains centered in Europe.

More important, many non-Caribbean states have significant political and economic interests in the Caribbean. In the early 1990s, France and Canada were deeply involved in international activities over the fate of Haiti and especially over the attempts to restore and consolidate Haiti's constitutional government. The Netherlands continues to play an important political and economic role in Suriname; it contributed to Suriname's gradual democratization in the early 1990s. The Russian Federation has extensive and important trade and financial relations with Cuba. Japan has significant stakes in the efficient flow of maritime traffic through the Panama Canal and the Caribbean sea-lanes. The European Union's preferential trading system, known from its founding document as the Lomé Convention, includes the former British and Dutch colonies of the Caribbean, plus, more recently, the Dominican Republic.

To be sure, the United States has preponderant political and economic power in the American Mediterranean, and through the Caribbean Basin

Initiative first approved in the early 1980s it has had its own preferential trading system. But the preeminence of the United States in these areas is markedly less decisive than in the military area, at least in part because since the early 1990s the U. S. government's budget crisis limited Washington's willingness and ability to exert greater economic power in the Caribbean.

A fair number of extra-regional international organizations provide considerable economic assistance and, as a result, wield somewhat autonomous political and economic clout. These include the International Monetary Fund, the World Bank, and the Inter-American Development Bank.

In short, at the political and economic level, the American Mediterranean, and especially the Caribbean, are not unipolar but polycentric. Many extra-regional states and some international organizations compete, cooperate, participate, and even intervene in the affairs of the region and within some of its countries. The relationship among these external powers is best called "polycentric" rather than "multipolar" because, for the most part, the various extra-regional powers (albeit with occasional exceptions) do not consciously seek to "balance" U. S. power and thereby create alternative poles of power; instead, the Europeans, Canadians, and Japanese pursue their interests on their own. Such interests are not necessarily at odds with those of the United States, but they are often different and at times competitive. In the 1990s, as in other times in the twentieth century, such polycentrism creates room for maneuver for the countries of the American Mediterranean. On this dimension, the present is not unlike the past.

"SMALL-ISLANDIST" IDEOLOGIES

At the attitudinal level, the countries of the American Mediterranean might be described (with some license) as islands with their backs to the sea and to each other. Their peoples and governments have long lived in the grip of what might be called "small-islandist" ideologies, namely, they exist and act as if oblivious to the presence of their neighbors and are often disdainful, suspicious, or hostile toward them. These ideologies, in turn, have a structural origin in the region's diverse and fragmented geography. To be sure, the ideologies endure for reasons beyond such structural factors, as they embody the identities, cultures, and histories of the peoples of each territory.

More technically, the "international subsystem" of the American Mediterranean has always depended on the behavior of extra-regional actors. The extra-regional actors have created this international subsystem and endowed it with much of its rhythm. Spain connected Cuba to Panama. England connected Guyana to Belize. The United States connected Puerto Rico to Nicaragua. And, as we shall see, the pirates of old and new have always brought the parts of the American Mediterranean into close contact with each other. The disconnection among the countries within the region meant that they were "price takers," not "price setters," of the very international subsystem in which they existed: the subsystem was shaped for them by outsider powers and by the pirates.

None of the Central American countries has its political, demographic, or economic epicenter on the Caribbean; their major cities are on mountain valleys or on the Pacific Ocean. It is principally the U. S. conception that Central America and the Caribbean are part of a "Caribbean Basin" that has forced elites in the two distinct subregions (Central America and the Caribbean) to focus specifically on each other. In the early 1980s, the Reagan administration's concerns over Cuba, Nicaragua, El Salvador, and Grenada, and its adoption of the Caribbean Basin Initiative as a preferential trading system, finally forced the governments and the businesses in the two subregions to realize that they were not just in the same "basin" but, alas, in the same "boat." They had to deal with each other in order to deal with the United States. And yet, the point remains that the countries of each of the two subregions did not "naturally" connect with each other.

Among the Caribbean Islands, the quite varied colonial heritage and the cultural and linguistic differences have kept the islands apart over the centuries.[3] Despite occasionally brave and invariably romantic talk, the Spanish and the Anglophone Caribbean might as well be on different planets, so limited has their formal state-to-state interaction been. Even within the Anglophone Caribbean, "small-islandism" has a powerful hold on the minds of people. The United Kingdom sought to grant independence to a Federation of the West Indies, which barely lasted about three years. Even weaker confederal efforts have had, at best, modest success. The independence of the micro-states of the eastern Caribbean is testimony to the power of small-islandist ideologies.

The Guianas and Belize might be described as islands surrounded mostly by land. This preposterous expression calls attention to the at times indifferent and hostile relations that these countries have with their Spanish- or Portuguese-speaking neighbors, and the Guianas with each other. Belize may be geographically part of Central America, but its society's cultural identity is located somewhere between Jamaica and Barbados.

Though the "island" metaphor is too strained to characterize such large countries as Venezuela and Colombia, they too had remarkably modest engagement with their near neighbors to the north until the 1970s. In the 1970s, the Venezuelan government became active throughout the Caribbean and Central America. In the 1980s, both Venezuela and Colombia played important and generally constructive roles in addressing the international and internal conflicts swirling in Central America. The "backs-to-sea" metaphor fits, however, one important feature of the bilateral Colombian-Venezuelan relationship. The 1943 treaty that was supposed to settle their boundary dispute dealt effectively enough with the land boundary, but it stopped at the water's edge. Their dispute over the demarcation of the waters and the deep seabed in the Gulf of Venezuela lingers into the 1990s.[4]

Small-islandist ideologies have impeded the concertation of political and economic efforts to advance the shared goals of the countries of the American Mediterranean. Over time, the fragmentation of the region has facilitated extra-regional influence and even intervention. There have always been subregional efforts at integration, especially within Central America and, separately, within the Anglophone Caribbean. In the 1990s, there are discernible attempts to strengthen these subregional integration efforts, but it is too early to tell whether such endeavors are but one more swing of a pendulum that will not stand still in the years ahead. On balance, therefore, there has been little change in the attitudinal legacies of the peoples of the American Mediterranean in terms of their relationships with each other.

BETWEEN GULLIVER AND THE LILLIPUTIANS: VENEZUELA AND CUBA

In the more recent history of the American Mediterranean, Cuba and Venezuela have sought to play an important role at the interstices of U. S. relations with the smaller countries of this part of the world.[5] Although the birth date of the American Mediterranean as an international subsystem is 1492, a plausible alternate birth date is 1958. In that year, Venezuela's democratic regime was founded; Batista fled Cuba, to be replaced by Fidel Castro's revolutionary government; and the United Kingdom granted independence to the West Indies Federation. Venezuela and Cuba acquired the distinctive regimes that would mark them for decades to come, and the soon-to-fragment West Indies Federation gave rise to the region's much more varied international political environment. (Relations between Venezuela, Cuba, and Central America are discussed in later sections.)

Venezuela's relations with the Anglophone Caribbean were instantly complicated, however, by its long-standing territorial dispute with British Guiana, which in 1966 became the independent country of Guyana. Venezuela claimed over half of Guyana's territory. A number of border clashes in the 1960s greatly increased the level of tension between Venezuela, on the one hand, and the Anglophone Caribbean that rallied to Guyana's side.[6] Difficulties in maritime boundary demarcation with Trinidad and Tobago added to Venezuela's troubled relations with the Anglophone countries. Since 1970, however, Venezuela has stepped back from pressing its territorial claims on Guyana and has developed more comprehensive and constructive relations with most of its northern near neighbors in search of joint gains from more cooperative relationships. Beginning on its own in the 1970s and, subsequently, jointly with Mexico in the 1980s, Venezuela has provided significant economic assistance to most independent countries in the Caribbean and Central America, helping them adjust to the energy price shocks of those times.

Cuba and the Anglophone Caribbean discovered each other in the early 1970s and proceeded to develop cordial relations.[7] By the end of the 1970s, Cuba's relations with Jamaica and Guyana had drawn much closer; in 1979, the New Jewel Movement's seizure of power in Grenada led to this country's close alignment with Cuba. Then, the tide turned. In the spring of 1980, the Cuban Air Force shot at and sank a Bahamian Coast Guard ship, killing four of its crew members. The radicalization of some Anglophone Caribbean politics, epitomized by Grenada's regime, frightened other governments. In the fall of 1983, Jamaica, Barbados, Dominica, St. Vincent and the Grenadines, St. Lucia, and Antigua asked for, and joined, the U. S. intervention to invade Grenada to overthrow its government. Though Cuban relations with its neighboring island governments have since improved, they have not reached again the intense cordiality that they briefly enjoyed.

Nonetheless, on this dimension too, the 1990s are not appreciably different than the years from the late 1950s to the late 1980s. In the 1990s, as before, Cuba and Venezuela seek to play roles between the United States and the other countries of the region. Their importance is clearly secondary to that of the United States; they often matter less than some other extra-regional powers. Two trends evident in the 1990s had been underway for many years. First, except for the 1979–1983 period, Cuba matters for the remainder of the Caribbean and, on balance, the relations are good, but Cuba is not a major factor in the region's international relations. Second, Venezuela's relations with the Caribbean have, for the most part, turned from adversarial to cooperative from the 1960s to the 1990s.

THE STRUCTURE OF THE CARIBBEAN'S INTERNATIONAL SUBSYSTEM—THE INFORMAL SECTOR

The "Unlawful" Movement of Peoples

"L'état, c'est moi." Though attributed to France's King Louis XIV, this is surely the motto of the millions of people from the Caribbean who have crossed international boundaries unlawfully. States cannot prevent illegal international migration in the Caribbean, despite their attempts to do so. Individuals act as though they were sovereign.

From every nook and cranny in the American Mediterranean people flock to the United States. The United States may have defeated Germany and, indirectly, the Soviet Union in the twentieth century, but it is almost powerless to stop the overflow of its borders. The Haitians, Jamaicans, Cubans, Salvadorans, Colombians, and Barbadians who live mainly along the eastern seaboard of the United States are a living testament to the resilience of the will to migrate, and to their enrichment of U. S. life.[8]

The migration that characterizes the American Mediterranean has multiple destinations, however. Haitians go to the Dominican Republic, Trinidadians to Venezuela, folks from all over the eastern Caribbean to Trinidad, as well as from island to island, Colombians enter Venezuela, Dominicans move to Puerto Rico, and so on. Caribbean peoples also have migrated in large numbers to the former metropolitan powers (the United Kingdom, France, and the Netherlands and, to some degree, Spain) and, more recently, to Canada. In this regard, surely the present is just like the past.

Quasi-State and Non-State Military Forces

From Sir Francis Drake to the late Colombian drug trafficker Pablo Escobar, quasi-state and non-state military leaders and their forces are a centuries-long feature of the American Mediterranean's international relations.[9] Since the sixteenth century, it has been useful to distinguish between the pirate and the privateer. The former was an autonomous agent, the latter was under some government's commission. In practice, the lines between them were often blurred. At war, governments commissioned pirates to become privateers; at peace, governments were often powerless to prevent privateers from returning to piracy. A characteristic thread connecting pirates and privateers was, of course, their pursuit of wealth.[10]

Quasi-state military forces in the twentieth century have been less motivated by wealth than by politics, however. The closest analogy to the privateers (minus the lust for wealth) are government-supported non-state military forces. In April 1961, the United States sponsored an exile invasion of Cuba; at other times in the 1960s, the U. S. government supported exile groups that attacked the Cuban government militarily. Throughout much of the 1980s, the U. S. government trained and funded military forces seeking to overthrow the government of Nicaragua. For its part, Cuba supported revolutionary activities in Venezuela in the 1960s, Nicaragua in the 1970s, El Salvador in the 1980s, and Guatemala and Colombia at various moments from the 1960s to the 1980s. As had been the case with privateers, neither Cuba nor the United States were always able to control those whom they had supported.[11]

Thus we find another change in the American Mediterranean that can be traced directly to the end of the cold war in Europe. In the 1990s, the United States and Cuba got out of the business of supporting non-state military forces in the region. The end of Soviet and eastern European support for Cuba, the collapse of Cuba's economy, and the breakup of the Soviet Union all contributed to the end of their individual and collective support for insurgencies throughout the American Mediterranean. With the Sandinista government's defeat in Nicaragua's 1990 elections, the United States also ended its support for insurgencies. In the early 1990s, quasi-state military forces have not been pertinent in this region.

Non-state military actors related to drug trafficking are very much pertinent, however. Because wealth motivates this behavior, the conceptual connection to the pirates of old is evident. The modern pirates matter because of their impact on the economies of the region, their corruption of government and society, and in some cases (especially but not limited to Colombia), their use of force to achieve their ends.

To fight pirates, major powers must commit their own military resources. The first U. S. military intervention anywhere in the world after the fall of the Berlin wall took place in 1989 in Panama, allegedly justified in part on the grounds that General Manuel Antonio Noriega's regime was involved with drug trafficking.[12] Since the early 1980s, U. S. military interventions might have been thinkable in the Bahamas and in Antigua, had their governments not taken steps to curtail drug traffic-related corruption and, in some instances, to punish government officials responsible for that corruption. In the Bahamas, the electorate replaced the government accused of such corruption. Fewer reforms have occurred in Antigua, which in 1989 played a role in the shipment of weapons to non-state military forces in Colombia: Vere Bird Jr., an Antiguan government minister and son of the prime minister, along with the chief of Antigua's army, facilitated the transshipment of arms and ammunition to a Colombian drug baron.[13]

At times, good police work and luck have saved the day. In the 1980s, the chief minister of the Turks and Caicos islands had the bad judgment of passing through Miami International Airport, where he was arrested by the FBI on the grounds of involvement with the drug traffic. In 1981, the government of Dominica's Prime Minister Eugenia Charles was saved by the good work of the FBI, which arrested would-be coup makers in New Orleans and confiscated their weapons.[14]

At one level, I am tempted to argue that the significance of non-state military forces is just one example of the centuries-long experience in the

American Mediterranean. And yet, by and large, piracy and privateering ended in this region early in the nineteenth century. Smuggling (with sporadic violence) was one legacy; it has been evident between Colombia and Venezuela, Trinidad and Venezuela, Haiti and the Dominican Republic, and among the various smaller islands. But smugglers did not typically command enough force to threaten established governments. The resurgent power of non-state military actors since the 1970s is novel enough in the history of the American Mediterranean, and it is a significant change.

The Rogue State and the Future of Military Intervention

To think about the future of military activity in the Caribbean, we should focus on the intersection between the formal and the informal international sectors to find a likely cause for war: the rogue state.

1. Suppose the government of one of the islands becomes more, not less, involved with drug traffickers and turns into an open haven for a drug cartel's financial, shipping, and military activities.

2. Suppose mere good police work cannot rescue other island governments from being overthrown by thugs.

3. Suppose an armed religious fundamentalist group seizes control of one of the Caribbean Islands, which almost happened in Union Island (part of St. Vincent and the Grenadines) in 1979 and in Trinidad in 1990.

In such instances, would the United States intervene militarily and unilaterally? Would the United States and other Caribbean governments intervene jointly, following the precedent of the 1983 intervention in Grenada? Would concerned governments call upon the United Nations or the Organization of American States? Or would they tolerate the sovereign majesty of the rogue state?

In the international environment created since the collapse of the Soviet Union, the prospects for collective international intervention against rogue states have risen. In this region in the early 1990s, the successful role of United Nations peace-making and peace-keeping forces in Nicaragua and El Salvador has increased the likelihood that collective intervention against rogue states would be considered normatively superior and empirically more effective. And the U. S. request to the United Nations Security Council for authorization prior to its intervention in Haiti in 1994 also increases the odds that collective intervention would be preferred to unilateral intervention.

THE STRUCTURE OF THE CARIBBEAN'S INTERNATIONAL SUBSYSTEM— TRANSNATIONAL AND SUPRANATIONAL ORGANIZATIONS

For the first time since Columbus blundered into the American Mediterranean, since the 1970s there have been international institutions with considerable clout seeking to shape the behavior and norms of conduct of the region's actors. Since the late 1970s, a consortium of international donors, coordinated by the World Bank, has played an important economic tutelary role over the governments of the Caribbean.[15] Since about the same time, the International Monetary Fund has exercised power and disbursed funds, also in a tutelary role, to stabilize the economies of various countries in this region.

In economic terms, business firms have long played a decisive role in the affairs of these countries. Their role has not changed appreciably in the recent past. The only noteworthy change is Cuba's economic self-rediscovery as a Caribbean country. In the early 1990s, its government opened the doors to international tourism and foreign direct investment.

Since the early 1990s, the United Nations has thrice played a military role in Central America, first in Nicaragua, then in El Salvador, and in 1997 in Guatemala. Moreover, Jean-Bertrand Aristide's reinstallation as president of Haiti in 1994 depended upon the deployment of U. S. and other international military and police forces to Haiti following a decision by the United Nations Security Council to authorize such use of force. Police officers from several Anglophone Caribbean countries joined the intervention.

Also since the early 1990s, under the authority of the 1991 Santiago Declaration, the Organization of American States (OAS) became much more actively committed to defend constitutional government and democracy. The OAS played an important role in mid-1993 in the reversal of a coup attempt in Guatemala. In 1994, OAS officials and election observers noted that substantial fraud had been committed in the presidential elections in the Dominican Republic and worked successfully with the U. S. government and others to persuade President Joaquín Balaguer to agree to shorten his new term from four years to two years; in 1996, Leonel Fernández was elected and inaugurated as president of the Dominican Republic. Since the overthrow of Haiti's President Aristide in 1991, the OAS labored to restore constitutional government to that country.

The nature of certain U. S. actions also has changed. As noted earlier, the Reagan administration's Caribbean Basin Initiative forced governments and firms from the Caribbean and Central America to increase the frequency and intensity of their contacts with each other. In effect, this international subsystem, created and sustained by external action, came at long last to involve direct relations among most of its actors.

Supranational activity also has quickened within the two main subregions. Since the late 1980s, steps have been taken to advance the level of economic integration within Central America and, separately, also within the Anglophone Caribbean. Through the Caribbean Community (CARICOM), the Caribbean Development Bank, the Organization of Eastern Caribbean States, the Eastern Caribbean Central Bank, and participation in the European Union's Lomé Convention, the Anglophone Caribbean has developed a thick, and often effective, network of supranational institutions. In 1995, CARICOM admitted Suriname to membership.

"THE NORMS OF "CIVILIZED CONDUCT"

In the sixteenth century, Spain sought to enforce a code of civilized conduct on the pirates who sacked its empire.[16] In the mid-nineteenth century, Great Britain sought to stop the international slave trade.[17] Throughout the nineteenth century, European powers sought to impose a code of civilized economic conduct on various states in the American Mediterranean, using force against Mexico and Venezuela for various purposes, including the collection of unpaid debts. In the early twentieth century, under the Roosevelt Corollary, the United States assumed this mission (along with debt collection); U. S. forces occupied Haiti, the Dominican Republic, Cuba, Puerto Rico, Nicaragua, and Panama for varying lengths of time.[18] In all such cases, the sword was clothed with moral purpose, but it remained a sword even though some moral purposes were served.

As the twentieth century closes, the world's international debt regime has changed; it has come to rely on non-military means of enforcement. In the 1990s, the international code of economic conduct is enforced through the multilateral agencies, especially the International Monetary Fund, the World Bank, and the Inter-American Development Bank, as well as through the United States. The international financial institutions are more cost-effective than gunboat diplomacy.

More than in the past, in the 1990s there also is an attempt to elicit, if one can, to impose, if one must, a code of civilized conduct in the relationships between states and their own society. The concerns for the respect for human rights and democracy address this issue.[19] These concerns understandably motivate many ordinary citizens. They motivate as well the lofty commitments of the American republics enshrined in the 1991 Santiago Declaration. But the application of these norms of conduct remains shaded by other concerns.

The U. S. government's treatment of human rights violations in Mexico, for example, is subdued and subordinate to a wider array of U. S. interests in Mexico. The U. S. government's concern with human rights and democracy in the case of Haiti has been variable. In 1981, the U. S.–Haitian migration agreement signaled that the only truly important U. S. concern in Haiti was to obtain the Haitian government's cooperation to stop the migration of Haitians to the United States.[20] The Clinton administration's interest in restoring constitutional government in Haiti had many noble components, but one important reason was to make it easier to assert that no Haitian fleeing to the United States has a reasonable fear of persecution and can, therefore, be safely sent back to Haiti.

On behalf of the new code of civilized conduct and through the instrument of the United Nations and the Organization of American States, the intervention in Haiti in 1994 was the first genuine[21] collective intervention in the Americas to depose one set of rulers and impose another ("restore" is the word international lawyers would use). There is nothing new about the significance of international norms in this international subsystem, but the enforcement of international norms through supranational institutions and collective action is certainly a pathbreaking departure.

In the 1990s, nowhere in this region are the issues of human rights and democracy more poignantly raised than in the case of Cuba, where the Cold War has not ended. There has been a deepening Latin American and Caribbean consensus about fostering Cuba's peaceful democratization. Such a consensus has been torpedoed by U. S. unilateralism. In the fall of 1992, the United States enacted the Cuban Democracy Act (CDA). Motivated in part by a genuine interest in human rights and democracy in Cuba, the CDA imposed sanctions on U. S. firms whose subsidiaries trade with Cuba from bases operating in third countries.

Not surprisingly, U. S. allies and trading partners in the Americas and elsewhere objected to the CDA. For the first time since the United States imposed its trade embargo on Cuba in 1960, in late 1992 the United Nations General Assembly condemned the U. S. embargo (only Israel and Rumania voted with the United States). The General Assembly voted in favor of this same motion by ever-growing majorities (the number of abstentions dropped each year) in subsequent years. In July 1993, the Iberoamerican Summit of Heads of Government called upon the United States to lift its embargo on Cuba.[22] Instead, in March 1996, the United States enacted the "Cuban Liberty and Democratic Solidarity Act," sponsored by Senator Jesse Helms and Representative Dan Burton, an act that imposed additional sanctions on countries that engage in economic relations with Cuba. The European Union, Canada, and various Latin American and Caribbean countries redoubled their efforts to stop such U. S. unilateral acts; in response, President Clinton waived the implementation of the most controversial features of this act. Nonetheless, these two acts remain obstacles to collective action on behalf of fostering peaceful changes toward democracy and human rights in Cuba.

CONCLUSIONS

The international relations of the American Mediterranean force us to be realistic but not "neorealists." The "units" of this international subsystem have never been just states.[23] Over the centuries, major powers have used military forces against each other and against local states, but states active internationally in this region have been bedeviled by the salience and clout of non-state actors. Some have been the pirates of old and new vintage. Others have been the firms that made the region suffer and glitter simultaneously. Nowhere else in the world are non-state actors so militarily, politically, and economically powerful; this trait marks the uniqueness of this international subsystem.

Despite these and other impressive continuities, three specific structural changes are evident in this international subsystem, as compared with its own long historical trajectory. First, the military hegemony of one power (the United States) is at last uncontested. Second, quasi-state military forces are no longer significant. Third, non-state military forces have become much more important than at any time since the Napoleonic Wars.

Structural and normative changes have combined to accord a new salience to the role of international institutions, which in the American Mediterranean help shape international and domestic events to a more significant degree than anywhere in the world outside of the European community.[24] No extracontinental power contests U. S. military power, and no alternate set of values contests the hegemonic preeminence of democracy and markets. But non-state military power—in the hands of the new pirates—has risen to challenge the power of the United States and its allies in local settings.

There have been two institutional responses to these structural changes. With regard to the economy, due to U. S. leadership and power, international institutions began to play tutelary roles in the late 1970s, and have done so ever since. A novelty of the 1990s has been the importance of international institutions to make and keep the peace and to overthrow rulers on behalf of democratic ideologies, constitutional government, and human rights, though not yet to fight the military power of non-state actors.

The disposition to collective intervention in the 1990s in the American Mediterranean (in Nicaragua, Trinidad and Tobago, El Salvador, Haiti,

and Guatemala) and the normative legitimacy that such action has acquired focus attention on the renewed political instability of several of the
region's governments. Will domestic crises in the region lead again and
again to collective international intervention in the domestic affairs of particular countries?

In 1990, the government of Trinidad and Tobago was nearly overthrown; its prime minister and several members of his cabinet were kid-
napped for several days. In 1991, the president of Haiti was overthrown.
In 1992, there were two (unsuccessful) coup attempts to overthrow the
president of Venezuela, who was impeached by constitutional means in
1993. In 1993, the president of Guatemala sought (unsuccessfully) to stage
a coup against the Congress, the courts, and the political parties. Cuba's
regime has become vulnerable to a considerable degree. In the late 1980s
and early-to-mid 1990s, disappointed electorates voted against long-
governing parties in Barbados, Jamaica, Guyana, Trinidad and Tobago,
and several of the smaller countries, and turned power over to opposition
parties (to be sure, these elections followed constitutional procedures, but
they reflect underlying anger nonetheless). Not since the early 1960s was
such political instability evident. The United States, now the militarily uncontested hegemon, and the newly empowered international institutions
may be busy in this part of the world in the years ahead.

Given the renewed political instability in the region, the possible rise
of rogue states, and the uncontested U. S. military primacy, the United
States is not likely to deny itself the right to intervene militarily in this region. The choice for the region is not between the presence and absence of
international coercion, but between forms and agents of coercion. The alternative to unilateral U. S. military intervention is to develop collective
means to protect constitutional governments under forcible assault from
criminal elements or from factions within their security forces. To ward off
unilateral U. S. intervention in the American Mediterranean, there must be
international institutions willing and able to act effectively in response to
the crises that lie over the horizon.

The international relations of the American Mediterranean are "thick"
and intense, because everyone can wield a gun—the powers, the pirates,
and even individuals—and because everyone can claim to act heir to traditions of centuries or on behalf of moral rights enshrined in the international community. Out of righteousness and war, there has emerged a
mixture of formality and informality within and across borders. Such is
the Caribbean: a combination of the beauty of its environment and the
fury of its hurricanes. Its paradoxes have marked its past and are likely to
shape its future.

NOTES

1. A first version of this essay was presented at the workshop on "The Caribbean and Cuba in the Post Cold-War," May 20–22, 1993, Caracas, Venezuela. The workshop was sponsored by the Woodrow Wilson Center of the Smithsonian Institution (Washington), the Centro de Estudios sobre América (Havana), and the Instituto Venezolano de Estudios Sociales y Políticos (Caracas). I am grateful to Joseph Tulchin, Rafael Hernández, and Andrés Serbin for the invitation to participate and for their comments. A second version of this essay was presented at a workshop on "Security and the Military in South America after the Cold War," June 4–5, 1993, University of California–San Diego. I am grateful to David Lake, Brian Loveman, and especially David Mares for the invitation and for their comments. The responsibility for errors is mine alone. An earlier version of this essay was published in *Cuba and the Caribbean: Regional Issues and Trends in the Post-Cold War Era*, ed. Rafael Hernández, Joseph Tulchin, and Andrés Serbin (Scholarly Resources, 1997). It is reprinted with permission.

2. For the evolution of U. S. hegemony in this region, see Dexter Perkins, *A History of the Monroe Doctrine* (Boston: Little, Brown and Co., 1963).

3. M. G. Smith, *The Plural Society in the British West Indies* (Berkeley: University of California Press, 1965).

4. John D. Martz, "National Security and Politics: The Colombian-Venezuelan Border," *Journal of Interamerican Studies and World Affairs* 30, no. 4 (winter 1988–89): 117–135; Larry George, "Realism and Internationalism in the Gulf of Venezuela," *Journal of Interamerican Studies and World Affairs* 30, no. 4 (winter 1988–89): 139–163.

5. For a history through the mid-1970s, see Robert Bond, ed., *Contemporary Venezuela and Its Role in International Affairs* (New York: New York University Press, 1977).

6. Leslie B. Rout Jr., *Which Way Out? A Study of the Guyana-Venezuela Boundary Dispute*, Monograph no. 4 (East Lansing, Mich.: Latin American Studies Center, Michigan State University, 1971).

7. For discussion, see Reginald Jones, "Cuba and the English-speaking Caribbean," in *Cuba in the World*, ed. Cole Blasier and Carmelo Mesa-Lago (Pittsburgh: University of Pittsburgh Press, 1979).

8. The Caribbean's two Nobel Prize winners, for example—the late Sir Arthur Lewis and Derek Wallcot—resided in the United States.

9. J. H. Parry, *The Spanish Seaborne Empire* (New York: Alfred A. Knopf, 1967).

10. For a succinct account of the history of piracy, see Jan Rogoziński, *A Brief History of the Caribbean* (New York: Facts on File, 1992), especially chapters 3, 7, and 8.

11. Cuban exiles once employed by the U. S. Central Intelligence Agency to fight the Castro government were among those caught in the Watergate scandal that eventually led to President Richard Nixon's resignation.

12. For a more general discussion, see Donald J. Mabry, ed., *The Latin American Narcotics Trade and U. S. National Security* (Greenwood Press, 1989).

13. Ron Sanders, "The Drug Problem: Policy Options for Caribbean Countries," in *Democracy in the Caribbean*, ed. Jorge I. Domínguez, Robert A. Pastor, and R. DeLisle Worrell (Baltimore: Johns Hopkins University Press, 1993).

14. Anthony Maingot, "The Internationalization of Corruption and Violence: Threats to the Caribbean in the Post-Cold War World," in *ibid.*

15. Robert A. Pastor, *Whirlpool: U. S. Foreign Policy toward Latin America and the Caribbean* (Princeton: Princeton University Press, 1992), 50, 177.

16. I am grateful to Joseph Tulchin for recalling this topic to my attention. All mistakes in understanding his insights are mine alone.

17. David Murray, *Odious Commerce: Britain, Spain, and the Abolition of the Cuban Slave Trade* (Cambridge: Cambridge University Press, 1980).

18. Dana G. Munro, *Intervention and Dollar Diplomacy in the Caribbean, 1900–1921* (Princeton: Princeton University Press, 1964).

19. For a critical assessment of this effort, see Lars Schoultz, *Human Rights and United States Policy toward Latin America* (Princeton: Princeton University Press, 1981).

20. Alex Stepick, "Unintended Consequences: Rejecting Haitian Boat People and Destabilizing Duvalier," in *Western Hemisphere Immigration and United States Foreign Policy*, ed. Christopher Mitchell (University Park, Penn.: Penn State University Press, 1992).

21. In 1965, the United States invaded the Dominican Republic allegedly to prevent the creation of a "second Cuba"; after the fact, the United States asked the Organization of American States to organize a collective intervention—in effect, to "launder" its unilateral act. For discussion, see Jerome Slater, *Intervention and Negotiation: The United States and the Dominican Revolution* (New York: Harper and Row, 1970). In 1983, the United States and several Anglophone Caribbean countries invaded Grenada to overthrow its government, allegedly in response to a request from the Organization of Eastern Caribbean States (OECS). But the OECS charter did not contemplate such action; moreover, OECS resolutions required unanimity, yet only four of the seven OECS members supported the invasion.

22. The Summit declaration mentioned neither the United States nor Cuba, but its meaning was unmistakable.

23. For a classic statement of the neorealist position, see Kenneth N. Waltz, "Theory of International Relations," in *Handbook of Political Science*, ed. Fred I. Greenstein and Nelson W. Polsby, vol. 8 (Reading, Mass: Addison-Wesley, 1975).

24. In some respects, Europe lags. The Eastern Caribbean Central Bank and the Eastern Caribbean dollar exemplify the common currency and the single multistate central bank that Europe has yet to fashion.

6

THE GEOGRAPHY OF DRUG TRAFFICKING IN THE CARIBBEAN

IVELAW L. GRIFFITH

The Caribbean lies at what Jóse Martí once called "the Vortex of the Americas," making it a bridge or front between North and South America. However, the region's strategic value lies not only in its geopolitical value, as viewed by state actors engaged in conflict and cooperation; over the last few decades, the region has also been viewed as being strategic by non-state drug actors, also with conflict and cooperation in mind, but in terms of geonarcotics, not geopolitics.

Geonarcotics is a concept developed to explain the multiple dynamics of the narcotics phenomenon. It posits that the phenomenon is multidimensional, with four main problem areas—production, consumption abuse, trafficking, and money laundering—and that these give rise to actual and potential threats to the security of states around the world. In addition, it suggests that drug operations and the activities to which they give rise precipitate conflict and cooperation among various state and non-actors in the international system. Over and above this, the term captures the dynamics of four factors—drugs, geography, power, and politics.

Geography is a factor because of the global spacial dispersion of drug operations and because certain geographic features facilitate some drug operations. Power involves the ability of individuals and groups to secure compliant action. This power is both state and non-state in source, and in some cases non-state sources exercise relatively more power than state entities. Politics, the fourth factor, revolves around resource allocation in the Lasswellian sense of the ability of power brokers to determine who gets what, how, and when. Since power in this milieu is not only state power, resource allocation is correspondingly not exclusively a function of state power holders. Moreover, politics becomes perverted, and all the more so where it already was perverted.[1]

This chapter focuses on trafficking, taking the work on geonarcotics one step further. Although production, consumption abuse, trafficking, and money laundering are all present in the Caribbean, it is trafficking that best highlights the region's strategic value, dramatizing the importance of geography as a geonarcotics factor. Much has been written about trafficking in the Caribbean, but there is as yet no assessment of the geography-trafficking nexus. Helping to fill this void here entails profiling the region geographically and examining the methods and patterns of trafficking.

THE CARIBBEAN AS VORTEX

Any discussion of the Caribbean as vortex should begin with what is perhaps the most dominant geographical feature of the region: the Caribbean Sea. The Caribbean Sea is 1,049,500 square miles in area. Its north-south width ranges from 380 to about 700 miles. The greatest depth of passage connecting the Eastern Caribbean with the Atlantic Ocean is the Anegada Passage, a sea lane of 48 nautical miles between the Anegada and Sombrero islands. The name "Caribbean" was introduced in 1773 by Thomas Jeffreys, author of *The West Indies Atlas*. He named the sea after the Carib people, who are native to many of the islands in the area. The islands in the Caribbean Sea form a chain almost 2,500 miles long, but never more than 160 miles wide, creating a bridge between North and South America.[2]

Both the physical and social geography of the Caribbean make it conducive to drug trafficking. Aspects of the former are more important than the latter, and in the physical geography area the key elements are island character and location.

Except for mainland Belize, French Guiana, Guyana, and Suriname (and Venezuela, Colombia, and the Central American states, if one is thinking of the Caribbean Basin), Caribbean countries are all island territories. Some are plural island territories, such as the Virgin Islands, consisting of about 100 islands and cays. Indeed, one—the Bahamas—is an archipelago of 700 islands and 2,000 cays. This island character permits entry into and use of Caribbean territories from scores, sometimes hundreds, of different places from the surrounding sea. For the mainland states, access is from various places from the Atlantic Ocean in the case of Guyana, Suriname, and French Guiana, and from the Caribbean coast in the case of Belize. And when one adds to the matrix the inability of Caribbean countries to provide adequate territorial policing, their vulnerability to trafficking is more readily appreciated.

The most important location feature of the region's physical geography is proximity. This proximity is dual: to South America, a major drug supply source, and to North America, a major drug consumer. On the supply side, the world's cocaine is produced in South America, coming notably from Colombia, Peru, Bolivia, Brazil, Ecuador, and Venezuela. Colombia alone produces about 80 percent of all of the cocaine in the world, although only about 20 percent of worldwide coca leaf cultivation is done there. (Colombia's coca cultivation is reported to have grown 13 percent in 1995, making that country the world's second largest coca producer, after Peru. Bolivia's place has now been reduced from second to third.) A significant proportion of global heroin and marijuana production also comes from South and Central America, especially from Colombia, Mexico, Peru, Paraguay, Brazil, and Guatemala.[3]

On the demand side, the United States has the dubious distinction of being the world's single largest drug-consuming nation. An analyst at the Congressional Research Service reported as follows in 1988: "America is consuming drugs at an annual rate of more than six metric tons (mt) of heroin, 70 to 90 mt of cocaine, and 6,000 to 9,000 mt of marijuana—80 percent of which are imported. American demand therefore is the linchpin of one of the fastest-growing and most profitable industries in the world."[4] By 1993, however, State Department estimates placed consumption of cocaine alone at 150 to 175 metric tons, valued at U.S. $15–17.5 billion.[5] In April 1995, General Barry McCaffrey, then head of the U. S. Southern Command, now the U. S. drug "czar," estimated that about 300 metric tons of the approximately 575 metric tons of cocaine available worldwide in 1994 were consumed in the United States.[6]

There is not much distance between either the Caribbean and South America, or between the Caribbean and the United States, especially the southern and northeastern parts of the United States. Some countries, like the Bahamas, Cuba, Haiti, Jamaica, and the Cayman Islands, are just a stone's throw away from Miami. Except for French Guiana and Suriname, all Caribbean countries are less than 2,000 miles from Miami. And only seven of them—Barbados, French Guiana, Grenada, Guyana, St. Vincent and the Grenadines, Suriname, and Trinidad and Tobago—are more than 2,000 miles from Atlanta and Washington, D. C. As for distances between the Caribbean and some main South American drug centers, twenty-four Caribbean countries are less than 1,000 miles from Caracas, and all except Belize (in relation to Caracas), French Guiana (in relation to Cali and Medellín), and Suriname (in relation to Medellín) are less than 1,500 miles away from Bogotá, Cali, Caracas, and Medellín.

These distances are calculated using air distances from Caribbean capitals and from international airport locations where non-capital cities are involved. Thus, what is masked is the reality that for some trafficking purposes the distances are often shorter, given the fact that there are places in some Caribbean territories, outside of the capitals, that are closer to United States or Latin American territory, and traffickers use this greater proximity. For example, Nassau is only 183 miles away from Miami, but Bimini is even closer—40 miles from the Florida Keys. A mere 90 miles separate Cuba from the United States. The distance between Port of Spain and Caracas is 371 miles. However, it is only miles between La Brea in southwestern Trinidad and Pedernales in northeastern Venezuela, a point called Serpent's Mouth. Moreover, the town of Lethem in southwest Guyana is a mere 75 miles away from the city of Boa Vista in northeast Brazil; and Eteringbang, Guyana, is only 28 miles from El Dorado, Venezuela.[7]

Europe is also a huge drug-consuming area, with cocaine, heroin, and marijuana imports coming through and from the Caribbean. However, despite the relatively great distance between that continent and the Caribbean region, the Caribbean is a major transit area for drugs bound for Europe. There are several explanations. One is the proximity between the Caribbean and South America. A second relates to commercial, communications, and other linkages between Europe and the Caribbean, which provide the institutional and other infrastructure for trafficking.

Third, because French Guiana, Guadeloupe, and Martinique are Départments d'Outre Mer (DOMs) of France, Anguilla, Bermuda, the British Virgin Islands, the Cayman Islands, and Montserrat, and the Turks and Caicos are British dependencies, and Bonaire, Curaçao, Saba, and St. Maarten are integral parts of the Kingdom of the Netherlands, there are certain customs, immigration, and transportation connections between these territories and their respective European "owners," which are exploited by traffickers. Some of the arrangements are similar to those involving the United States and Puerto Rico and the U. S. Virgin Islands, which also facilitate traffickers aiming for destinations in the continental United States.

Each of the two physical geography elements—island character and location—can by itself be conducive to trafficking. However, the region's vulnerability to trafficking and the prospects for continued trafficking can be better appreciated when it is recognized that these factors are often mutually supporting and reinforcing and that they interact with aspects of social geography, which will be noted later. One way to understand the geography dynamics involved is to examine trafficking patterns and the modus operandi of traffickers.

TRAFFICKING PATTERNS AND ROUTES

Apart from shipping their own marijuana in the United States, some Caribbean countries are important transshipment centers for South American cocaine, heroin, and marijuana bound for Europe and North America.

For more than two decades, the Bahamas, Belize, and Jamaica dominated this business. The geography of the Bahamas makes it an excellent candidate for drug transshipment, given its hundreds of islands and thousands of cays and its strategic location in the airline flight path between Colombia and South Florida. Anthony Maingot once observed, "In a way, geography had always been the Bahamas' main commodity, and they had always marketed it with great skill."[8] This, of course, is true of other countries.

While most of the Bahamanian islands could be used for drug smuggling, the trade has been concentrated over the years in a few strategic places.[9] For a typical cocaine trafficking mission, aircraft depart from the north coast of Colombia, arriving in the Bahamas four to five hours later. The cargo is dropped either to waiting vessels or for later collection to be placed on vessels, then the final run is made to a U. S. point of entry. However, this is not the only trafficking method. Recently, traffickers have been employing other tactics, including the use of Cuban waters to evade OP-BAT (Operation Bahamas and the Turks and Caicos) measures, drop-offs by aircraft making only momentary landings, and development of a cocaine route through Jamaica.[10] Cocaine seizures dropped from 490 kilos in 1994 to 390 kilos in 1995, while marijuana seizures increased dramatically from a 1994 figure of 1,420 kilos to a 1995 figure of 3,530 kilos.[11]

The Bahamas has also become (in)famous for marijuana and hashish traffic, from South America as well as Jamaica. In fact, when the Bahamas first became a transshipment center, the drug involved was mainly marijuana, with a few consignments of hashish.[12] There is evidence of drug trafficking dating to 1968, when 250 to 300 pounds of marijuana were flown from Jamaica to Bimini. One of the earliest cocaine seizures was made in 1974: 247 pounds of pure cocaine, with a 1974 street value of U. S. $2 billion, at an airport in George Town, Exuma. That same year, the Bahamas police discovered off Grand Bahama a store of marijuana over six feet high and more than two miles long.[13]

There have been undulating patterns of drug seizures since the mid-to-late 1980s, reflecting variation in use of different countries by traffickers, successful countermeasures, and consequent trafficker adaptations. There are also, understandably, fluctuations in the number of people arrested. The following is a sample of the arrest figures reported in various editions of the *International Narcotics Control Strategy Report* (*INCSR*): the

Bahamas—1,373 in 1990, 1,500 in 1991, 1,135 in 1992, 1,023 in 1993, 1,025 in 1994, and 1,565 in 1995; Belize—658 in 1991, 1,529 in 1992, 1,287 in 1993, and 1,227 in 1994; Haiti—155 in 1990, 170 in 1991, 52 in 1993, and 107 in 1994; Jamaica—5,432 in 1990, 5,027 in 1991, 1,149 in 1992, 1,416 in 1993, 886 in 1994, and 3,705 in 1995. In all cases, both foreigners and locals were arrested. In the Bahamian case, Americans were always the largest group of foreigners, followed by a combination of Jamaicans, Colombians, and Haitians. However, there is also trafficking by nationals of places far away from the Bahamas. For example, in August 1990, a Nigerian woman was given a seven-year sentence by the Bahamian Supreme Court following her arrest in 1989 for attempting to smuggle 4.1 pounds of heroin and 1.25 pounds of cocaine out of the country.[14]

The geography and topography of Belize also make that country ideal for drug smuggling. Apart from a long coastline and contiguous borders with Guatemala and Mexico, two major heroin and marijuana producers, there are dense unpopulated jungle areas and numerous inland waterways. Moreover, there are about 140 isolated airstrips and virtually no radar coverage beyond a thirty-mile radius of the international airport at Belize City. While there is still air trafficking, recently there has been an increased use of maritime routes.

Crack has also been featuring more prominently. According to the 1994 *INCSR*, "for the first time [in 1993], there was evidence of Belizean export of crack cocaine to the United States."[15] Belize officials agreed with the U. S. government assessment in 1992 that the country's "growing importance as a transshipment point for South American cocaine is now the(ir) most important narcotics-related challenge."[16] That assessment has remained credible over the ensuing years. Indeed, while 141 kilos of cocaine were seized in 1994, two seizures in January 1995 alone netted 636 kilos. The overall 1995 cocaine seizures amounted to 840 kilos.[17]

Jamaica has long been key to the drug trade, given its long coastline, its proximity to the United States, its many ports, harbors, and beaches, and its closeness to the Yucatan and Windward Passages. Trafficking takes place by both air and sea. For the maritime traffic, use is often made of pleasure boats with storage compartments to ferry small quantities of drugs. Large loads are put aboard commercial cargo, pleasure, and fishing vessels. Both large and small amounts also are smuggled by air. Jamaica Defense Force (JDF) sources indicate that both legal and illegal airstrips are used for trafficking. The JDF was aware in December 1994 of forty-nine illegal airstrips, about 50 percent of which were capable of being brought into operational use. Many of the illegal airstrips are only 1,200 to 1,500 feet long, just long enough for Pipers, Cessnas, BE-100, and KingAir aircraft.

Jamaica's west and south coasts are the most popular areas for air trafficking. Apart from landings on strips designed or adapted for drug operations, landings are made on roads, in cane fields, and on legal strips owned by bauxite and sugar companies. The JDF has destroyed some eighty illegal airstrips and fields (up to December 1994), but as the JDF chief of staff explained, given the heavy limestone in many of the popular landing areas, operators are often able to make fields serviceable within ten days of destruction.

Most of the aircraft recovered from forced landings or after crashes are leased craft with U. S. registration, but most of the pilots are Bahamian or Bahamas-based. JDF officials expressed frustration that most of the time the aircraft are recovered by the owners using legal and administrative technicalities and loopholes. Planes now rarely come to a complete stop for trafficking operations. Loading and unloading is done by people called loaders, who run along the aircraft, putting on or taking off the cocaine and / or marijuana. Partly because of this, unless there is a crash, pilots are rarely caught; the loaders are the ones arrested.

Most of the cocaine air operations using Jamaica over the last few years have involved San Andres and Bogotá in Colombia, the Bahamas, Panama, and Curaçao. Traffickers do not rely only on illegal flights; legal commercial flights also are used. Particularly popular, and problematic for Jamaican officials, was the commercial link between San Andres and Montego Bay. That connection was severed in September 1994, but there are still commercial flights linking Jamaica and Colombia. Now, according to military intelligence sources, the drugs go from San Andres to Bogotá, and then to Montego Bay or Kingston.[18]

Marijuana seizures in 1993 included 75 metric tons, up from 35 metric tons the previous year. The actual amount of cocaine seized in 1993 was 160 kilograms, down from a 1992 high of 490 kilograms. The 1992 figure was exceptional because of one dramatic operation where 412 kilograms were confiscated. Heroin and hashish oil continue to be transshipped, with confiscations of the latter totaling 235 kilograms in 1993. There were 1,416 arrests in 1993, up by 267 from the 1992 figure of 1,149. According to the 1995 *INCSR*, during 1994, 179 kilos of cocaine, 47 kilos of hashish oil, and 1 kilo of heroin were seized, and 886 people were arrested for drug trafficking (and production). On March 3, 1995, a seizure occurred involving 10,000 pounds of marijuana, valued at $J 20 million. Three days later, another large confiscation took place: 4,000 pounds of marijuana, along with weapons and ammunition.[19]

Although the Bahamas, Belize, and Jamaica are still important drug trafficking centers, countermeasures there and in South and Central America have prompted traffickers to seek and develop alternative routes, bringing eastern and southern Caribbean countries into greater prominence since the early 1990s. The shifts are of such a magnitude that in November 1994 Puerto Rico and the U. S. Virgin Islands were designated by United States authorities as High-Intensity Drug Trafficking Areas (HIDTAs), a designation surely appropriate to other areas in the region. Moreover, because of the increased drug activity, in July 1995, the Drug Enforcement Administration (DEA) upgraded its presence in Puerto Rico from "Office" to Field Division, increasing its staffing and assigning a special agent—Félix Jiménez—to oversee the Caribbean, which was formerly done from Miami. The Division became operational on October 1, 1995.

In Barbados, for instance, a joint army police interdiction operation on July 4, 1992, confiscated over 2,000 pounds of marijuana, worth about B $6 million, and arrested two Barbadians and one Canadian with arms and ammunition. Later that month, 26.5 kilos of cocaine, worth about TT $35 million, were seized at Cali Bay, Tobago, following transshipment from Venezuela. Three couriers were caught in 1993 trying to use Barbados to transport Colombian heroin from Venezuela to Europe. Cocaine seizures in Barbados during 1994 amounted to 240 kilos, and the marijuana confiscated totaled 464 kilos.

In January 1993, 2,761 pounds of cocaine—worth some U. S. $17 million—were seized in St. Vincent following a raid on a family residence in Glamorgan, just outside of Kingstown. St. Vincent is now described by the U. S. government as "a pipeline for drugs transiting to the U. S. and French Islands." The report by the St. Vincent government of a mere 2.5 kilos of cocaine and 881 kilos of marijuana as 1994 seizures is considered by both U. S. and Caribbean observers a gross undercount. In Antigua, over 150 kilos of cocaine bound for the United Kingdom were seized on a private boat during the spring of 1994. Later that year, 130 kilos of cocaine, 169 pieces of crack, and 3,380 kilos of marijuana also were confiscated. Seizures declined in 1995: 110 kilos of cocaine, 217 kilos of marijuana, and 142 lieces of crack.[20]

In February 1993 alone, 3,240 kilos of ganja with an estimated street value of U. S. $16.2 million were recovered from waters around the British Virgin Islands.[21] Trinidad and Tobago had its biggest single cocaine seizure on June 10, 1994, when a 41-foot cabin cruiser, *Aquarius*, was intercepted with 226.2 kilos of cocaine, worth an estimated U. S. $18 million, in plastic fuel drums. The cruiser was bound for Antigua. Three Antiguans were arrested and later indicted on conspiracy and trafficking charges. From January to November 1995, in Trinidad and Tobago, 110 kilos of cocaine were seized (compared to 311 kilos in 1994), and 246 people were arrested for cocaine trafficking.[22]

In the U. S. Virgin Islands, 860 pounds of cocaine worth about U. S. $10 million were seized on August 25, 1994. That same month, two seizures in St. Martin netted 2,185 pounds of cocaine, and two months later, fishermen found 1,766 pounds of cocaine on an uninhabited island between St. Barthelemy and St. Martin. (Of the total 1994 cocaine seizure, out of 1.2 metric tons in the French Caribbean, 990 kilos were taken in St. Martin alone.) Added to that, in November 1994, 1,320 pounds of cocaine were seized in Guadeloupe. Elsewhere among the dependencies, 1994 seizures included: Anguilla—832 kilos of cocaine, 75 rocks of crack, and 28 kilos of marijuana; Cayman Islands—5 kilos of cocaine, 25 kilos of hashish oil, and 1.8 metric tons of marijuana; Turks and Caicos Islands—45 kilos of cocaine, 160 rocks of crack, and 15 kilos of marijuana. In January 1995, 742 pounds of marijuana were recovered off of the Cayman Islands. The drugs were in burlap sacks with the words "brown sugar made in Jamaica."[23] In January 1996, while operating near Grand Cayman, the British Frigate HMS *Brave* recovered U.S. $200 million worth of cocaine that had been dumped at sea earlier. Altogether, there were 3,000 pounds of cocaine in forty bales.[24] Overall, for the Cayman Islands in 1995, 548 people were arrested for trafficking, and the drugs confiscated included: 314 kilos of cocaine and 2.6 metric tons of marijuana.[25]

Aruba and the Netherlands Antilles are said to serve as vital links in the transshipment of cocaine and heroin from Colombia, Venezuela, and Suriname to the United States and Europe. The ABC islands (Aruba, Bonaire, and Curaçao) are very close to Venezuela, from which much of the drugs confiscated in ABC come. Trafficking in the Dutch Caribbean generally involves the use of commercial and private airlines, air cargo flights, and cruise ships, although ship containers also have been used. In Suriname, for example, in 1994, one seizure alone netted 207 kilos of cocaine concealed in cargo waiting to be shipped to Europe. Seizures in Aruba for 1995 totaled 153 kilos of cocaine, 366 kilos of marijuana, and 4 kilos of heroin; in the Netherlands Antilles, the figures were 111 kilos of cocaine, 810 kilos of marijuana, and 8 kilos of heroin.[26]

Cuba's strategic location has caused it to be used for trafficking, apparently both with and without official sanction. One 1983 DEA report dates official Cuban involvement to 1991, suggesting that there were economic and political motives involved. Cuban officials have often been indicted in the United States for trafficking. One of the earliest cases of importance was in November 1982, when four senior officials were convicted *in absentia*: Rene Rodriguez Cruz, of Dirección General de Inteligencia, Cuba's intelligence service, then also a Cuban Communist Party Central Committee member; Vice Admiral Aldo Santamaría Cuadrado, also a Central Committee member; Fernando Ravélo Renédo, former ambassador to Colombia; and Gonzalo Bassols Suarez, a former minister counselor of the Cuban embassy in Colombia. Ravélo Renédo and Basols Suarez reputedly directed arms-for-drugs deals involving the Medellín cartel and Colombia's M19.[27]

Andres Oppenheimer asserts that Fidel Castro and Colombian drug operators once had a long association, based mainly on political convenience. Castro is said to have first ordered his intelligence agencies to penetrate the Colombian drug networks in the 1970s to gain access to what then appeared as potentially one of Latin America's most powerful economic and political forces. Indeed, he says, "When the Carter administration launched exploratory dialogue with the Castro regime in the late 1970s, one of the things the Cubans offered was to help stop drug smuggling through the Caribbean. The proposal died when normalization talks collapsed."[28]

Cuban involvement in trafficking and questions about officially sanctioned involvement commanded the greatest attention in 1989, when several top military officials were convicted and given harsh sentences for trafficking, corruption, and other infractions. The chief defendant was Division General Arnaldo Ochoa Sanchez, then a hero of Cuba's Africa campaigns, who had in 1984 been awarded Cuba's highest military honors: Hero of the Cuban Republic, and the Máximo Gomez Order, First Class. All fourteen defendants were found guilty. Ochoa, Captain Jorge Martinez Valdez, Colonel Antonio De La Guardia, and Major Amado Padrón were sentenced to death. Brigadier General Patricio De la Guardia and Captain Miguel Ruiz Poo were each given thirty years in prison, and the eight others were given prison terms ranging from ten to thirty years.[29]

Several analysts indicate that the participation of military officials in the smuggling of drugs and other commodities was not done mainly to profit individual officers, but to satisfy the economic needs of the military in particular, and the economic and political interests of Cuba in general. Evidence suggests that both the military and the Cuban Communist Party knew about the trafficking and protected officials for some time, but turned on them when it became politically inexpedient to continue their operations. Oppenheimer claims, for instance, that "In 1988, the Commandante had asked [Interior Minister Division General Jose] Abrantes to sell 10 thousand kilos of cocaine that was in storage at Havana's Cimeq Hospital, if possible through Eastern European countries. Abrantes was to seek $50 million for the cocaine, which originated largely from Cuban coast guard seizures."[30]

Ever since the Ochoa affair, there have been periodic allegations of the collusion of Cuban officials in drug trafficking. In July 1996, for example, there was a claim that Fidel Castro himself had been deeply implicated in the attempt to smuggle 5,828 pounds of cocaine seized the previous January, a claim that of course the Cuban authorities denied.[31] But although there is no hard evidence of present Cuban government involvement in trafficking, there is considerable evidence of trafficking involving Cuba.

In April 1992, for example, twenty-nine Cubans in the city of Camaguey were found guilty of possessing and trafficking cocaine. Some were also convicted of currency and weapons possession charges.[32] Cuban officials reported that 3.3 metric tons of cocaine were seized in seventy-nine different cases during 1993. Reported seizures for 1994 included 238 kilos of cocaine and 1.1 metric tons of marijuana.[33] Cuba's national prosecutor is reported to have said the following in a November 1995 interview with *Granma*: "Years ago since this merchandise had no commercial value [in Cuba], everybody who found a packet of this type handed it over to the authorities. Now people have discovered how much that's worth and they don't always hand it over."[34]

Several features of the Dominican Republic also make that country a prime trafficking candidate: its proximity to Colombia, the Bahamas, Puerto Rico, and the southern United States; a long, often desolate, border with Haiti; and poorly equipped police and military authorities. Among other things, offshore air drops are often made between the Dominican Republic and Puerto Rico, and drugs are smuggled over the border from Haiti using the same techniques, routes, and resources used to smuggle petroleum into Haiti during the embargo. The scope of their problem is reflected in the fact that in 1993 the country's National Drug Control Directorate, supported by the navy, seized 1,073 kilograms of cocaine, 305 kilograms of marijuana, 1,444 grams of crack, and other drugs. Also confiscated were 183 vessels, 222 motorcycles, and 164 firearms. These were the results of 812 anti-drug operations where 5,635 people were arrested. In 1994, the seizures included 2.8 metric tons of cocaine (a 160 percent increase over 1993) and 6.8 metric tons of marijuana, and arrests numbered 3,000. In 1995, cocaine seizures climbed to 3.6 metric tons.[35]

In Haiti, the complicity of military and other officials has been well established.[36] The DEA estimated in 1993, for instance, that two to four tons of cocaine then passed through Haiti, mostly with the blessings of military officials. In April 1994, Gabriel Toboada of the Medellín cartel told a U. S. Senate Foreign Relations Committee hearing that Lt. Col. Joseph Michel François, then commander of Haiti's police, collaborated in the shipment of tons of cocaine during the 1980s. According to the testimony, the deal had been sealed in 1984 following François's visit to Medellín. Haiti was used as a bridge to the United States, with both the flights and the cargo protected by the military.[37]

Several factors explain Haiti's trafficking vulnerability and involvement: geographic location, poorly monitored coasts, mountainous interior, about twenty unpatrolled airstrips, inadequate law enforcement resources, and corruption. Officially reported cocaine seizures have been increasing recently. In 1992, the figure reported was 56 kilos of cocaine; in 1993, 157 kilos; and in 1994, 716 kilos.[38]

The return to power of Jean-Bertrand Aristide in October 1994 was expected to lead to reduced trafficking as the government reduced the size and role of the military in society and tried to deal with the problem of corruption. It is already clear that these actions are certainly not enough to combat Haiti's involvement in trafficking. Indeed, the post-intervention reconstruction itself negatively affected counternarcotics efforts. For example, the disbanding of the army, which occurred between November 1994 and April 1995, affected the functioning of the counternarcotics units: the National Narcotics Service (SSN) and the Combined Information and Coordination Center (CICC), which had been part of it. Thus, it was remarkable that Haitian authorities were able to seize over 550 kilos of cocaine during 1995.[39]

In the context of trafficking adaptation, Guyana has become an important center of operations. Like many other Caribbean countries, Guyana's trafficking use saw its graduation from marijuana to cocaine and heroin. The earliest known trafficking case was on June 16, 1979, when a trader from the bauxite mining city of Linden arrived from Jamaica with sixty pounds of compressed marijuana.[40] Cocaine and some heroin now enter Guyana from all three neighboring countries: Brazil, Suriname, and Venezuela. Data from the Guyana military and police show that cocaine seizures went from 127 grams, with twenty-two arrests, in 1990, to 7 kilos, with forty arrests, in 1991.

Cocaine seizures in 1993 were 463 kilos—1,000 percent higher than in 1992. The exceptional 1993 figure was due to one dramatic seizure, where on June 4, 1993, 800 pounds of cocaine were dropped from air into the Demerara River, along with U. S. $24,000, and huge quantities of Colombian and Guyanese currency. Several Guyanese, Colombians, and Venezuelans were implicated in the affair.[41] In 1994, the amount of cocaine confiscated dropped to 76 kilos, but 252 people were arrested for cocaine trafficking. The smaller amount seized should not create any sense of security, since this does not necessarily indicate a lessening of the quantity being trafficked. As one assessment concluded, "It may be the result of more sophisticated techniques and coordination on the part of drug smugglers or an insufficient drug enforcement unit."[42] There is reason to believe that both of these and other factors explain the smaller seizures in 1994, as well as in 1995, when only 51 kilos of cocaine were seized.

As with Jamaica, Trinidad and Tobago, Suriname, and elsewhere in the region, marijuana trafficking also exists. Both foreign and local marijuana are involved, the foreign marijuana coming from Colombia, Venezuela, and Brazil. According to military sources in Guyana, during 1994 alone, 56,707 kilos of marijuana were confiscated, up from 15,654 kilos seized in 1993. And on January 4, 1995, 5,000 pounds of marijuana valued at U. S. $2 million were discovered behind a false fiberglass wall of a container about to be shipped from Georgetown to Miami.[43]

The air, sea, and land routes developed for smuggling contraband into Guyana from Brazil, Venezuela, and Suriname during the economic crisis of the 1970s and 1980s have now been adapted for narcotics trafficking. A further complication is the fact that the borders with these countries are very long: 1,120 kilometers with Brazil; 745 kilometers with Suriname; and 600 kilometers with Suriname. Moreover, traffickers are able to take advantage of the country's large size (214,970 km^2), the coastal habitation, and the absence of adequate manpower and equipment to police the territory. In relation to air trafficking, for example, there are ninety-two legal aerodromes (private and public), most of them in remote parts of the country where the physical and social geography provides clear advantages for traffickers. One top military official conceded that "very often we do know what's happening in the some of those places."[44] And this was in relation to the legal airstrips.

The physical geography of Guyana—especially the size and location aspects—clearly facilitates trafficking. However, the role of social geography is noteworthy. In that respect, the country's demographics are important. Not only is there a low population density—three-quarters of a million people on 214,970 km^2 of territory—but most of the people live along the Atlantic Coast. This leaves vast expanses of territory both underpopulated and underpoliced, thus providing excellent scope for trafficking and other illegal operations. (Incidentally, this social geography of low density and coastal habitation is also found in Belize [Caribbean coast], French Guiana, and Suriname.)

Given the country's physical and social geography and the corruptibility of some officials, traffickers sometimes aim at establishing their own physical base in a big way. In one case, some Colombians and Americans were able to enter the country illegally and bring a generator, water pump, two airplane engines, six transmitting sets, tool kits, arms, ammunition, and other supplies over a four-month period. The plan was to build a processing and transshipment center at Waranama, in northeastern Guyana, 400 miles from the capital, Georgetown, to be part of an international network involving Colombia, Guyana, Trinidad and Tobago, and the United States.[45]

Like elsewhere in the Caribbean, trafficking in Guyana is not done only by runs dedicated to drug delivery or collection; commercial flights also are used. In one dramatic case, on March 15, 1993, a Guyana Airways Corporation (GAC) plane—flight GY 714—arrived in New York from Guyana with 117 pounds of cocaine in its panelling. The U. S. Customs imposed a fine of U. S. $1.8 million for this violation, which led the GAC to offer a million-dollar (Guyana) reward for information leading to the arrest and successful prosecution of the people involved in the affair.[46] This was the first time a Caribbean airline had been forced to resort to such desperate and dramatic action to deal with commercial trafficking. The case is yet to be solved.

Guyana's physical geography also makes it vulnerable to maritime trafficking. One could readily appreciate this when it is noted that Guyana, whose name is derived from an Amerindian word that means "Land of Many Waters," has hundreds of inland rivers and creeks. Thirteen huge rivers flow into the Atlantic Ocean. One—the Essequibo—is 667 miles long. Each of the rivers has a network of tributaries. The maritime traffic also is facilitated by the fact that the network of rivers also runs into Brazil, Suriname, and Venezuela. For example, the Takatu River in southwest Guyana flows into the Parima, a tributary of the Rio Negro, which flows into the Amazon in Brazil.

The Guyana situation is clear evidence of the vulnerability of Caribbean countries to drug trafficking and other operations. Geography apart, a contributor to this situation is the absence of adequate military and police resources to offer credible countermeasures. In effect, the state lacks the power to exercise proper political and territorial jurisdiction over the nation. Top army, coast guard, and police officials in many parts of the region have expressed frustration at not only the inability to adequately protect their countries' borders against trafficking, but also at being the pawns of traffickers who often create successful small interdiction diversions to execute large operations.[47]

CONVEYANCE AND ORGANIZATION

Drug trafficking brings out the creativity and ingenuity of drug operators and the people who collude with them. People have used every possible orifice of the human anatomy, every possible piece of clothing, all manner of fruits and vegetables, and a variety of craft, furniture, and other things for the conveyance of drugs. Insofar as the human anatomy is concerned, use has been made of the vagina, anus, arm pits (to strap packages of drugs), the abdomen and back (to strap packages), the tongue (by placing drugs under it), natural and false hair, thighs (where drugs are strapped on inner thighs), and the stomach and intestines. Indeed, there are people—called swallowers or mules—who specialize in the use of the stomach and intestines. In one spring 1996 case, a twenty-seven-year-old Jamaican-born U. S. permanent resident, Herman McGregor, packed sixty-six cocaine-filled balloons in his stomach in Montego Bay, Jamaica, and brought them to Miami on February 27, 1996. McGregor recounted how he had used porridge and milk in the ingestion process, but was unable to "flush" all of the balloons out of his intestines. He later became ill and sought medical treatment at the Florida Medical Center. The remaining balloons were discovered during the medical examination. They had to be removed surgically, during which process the police waited outside of the operating room to collect the evidence for prosecution.[48]

One Eastern Caribbean official related a case where a leg wound was used. Condoms with cocaine were found in the wound and within its bandages. Drugs have also been found in fish, rice, cake, pepper sauce, coconuts, cricket bats, yams, bananas, butter, cans of fruit, beer, and juice, cigarette packaging (purported to be cigarettes), cloth, vegetables, detergent, furniture and furniture fixtures, piñatas, false legs (of amputees), mail (letters, packages, and mail bags themselves), ceramic tiles, bottles of shampoo and mouthwash, videotapes, concrete posts, wooden coat hangers, rum (where liquid cocaine was purported to be coconut rum), and countless other objects. All sorts of clothing are used, including footwear with false soles and heels. Also used are picture frames and suitcases with false sides and bottoms.

Both dead and live birds and animals also are used to convey drugs. In one incredible case, dead cocaine-filled eviscerated parrots were found among a shipment of live parrots sent from Grenada to China in 1991.[49] One official recounted a situation where a guitar was made entirely of compressed marijuana. I call it "the case of the guitarganja." Not only are cars, vans, trucks, planes, and boats used to convey large and small quantities of drugs and people and objects with them, but drugs are often concealed in unbelievable places in these vessels: in car batteries and tires; in the panelling and upholstery of planes, boats, cars, trucks, and vans; in false boat hulls and bottoms; in false gas tanks of cars, vans, and trucks; in the gas itself; in false floors and walls of trucks and vans; and in ship containers, some with false sides and bottoms, some without.

Apart from risking discovery and prosecution, some traffickers risk physical injury and even death. Swallowers, for example, risk both, although they often drink coconut or olive oil to line the stomach and intestines before swallowing the condoms with cocaine, heroin, or compressed marijuana. As a matter of fact, scores of them have died when packages broke in their stomachs or intestines. Breakages occur for various reasons, including physiological reactions, improper packaging, and flight delays that cause the retention of drugs beyond the safe period, which it-self varies from drug to drug. In one dramatic March 1994 case in Jamaica, a trafficker died from a combination of factors, but most notably from the huge quantity of drugs ingested. The autopsy found that he had ingested 275 packets of compressed ganja, weighing about two pounds, which caused his stomach to literally explode.[50]

Traffickers are not only creative, but also are adaptive, changing methods and operatives depending on the success of counternarcotics measures. Hence, some of the methods mentioned earlier are used for a while, then changed. Some are used on a rotation basis, or in different routes. Often, some methods have just a one- or two-time use. Adaptations also take place in relation to trafficking routes. Indeed, the fact that Trinidad, Guyana, and Eastern Caribbean countries began to be used heavily after 1990 reflects changed route patterns. As was observed by the U. S. State Department, successful U. S. interdiction in the Bahamas and Turks and Caicos Islands, and U. S. military activity around Hispaniola, have contributed to the increased use of the Eastern Caribbean, Puerto Rico, and the U. S. Virgin Islands, such that "In 1994, 26 percent of docu-mented cocaine smuggling attempts into the U.S. came through these Caribbean portals."[51]

Most of the trafficking reflects careful planning and organization by people who are either fully aware of their role, or suspect that they are in-volved, but because of the need-to-know modus operandi are not sure of the extent of their involvement. Sometimes, though, people are unsus-pecting "mules," often under the impression that they are doing a favor for a friend, an associate, or even a lover. For example, as the Director of the Narcotics Trial Bureau in the Queens District Attorney's Office, New York, explained, countless gullible Caribbean (and other) women are duped by men who profess love and offer them the prospect of all-expense-paid trips to the United States, or an opportunity to emigrate there. When they make the trip(s) they are given packages to deliver to "friends" or "family" in the United States, only to later discover when ar-rested that they were merely being used to traffic drugs.[52]

As might be expected, given the profitability and lure of drug traf-ficking, not only "ordinary people" are involved or implicated, but mem-bers of the region's political, social, and corporate elite also have been involved. A few examples will suffice. One early case involved Chief Min-ister Norman Saunders and Commerce and Development Minister Stafford Missick of the Turks and Caicos Islands. They were arrested in March 1985 by United States authorities and charged with conspiracy to import narcotics in the United States, among other things. They were sentenced to eight and ten years, respectively, and each was fined U. S. $5,000. The following year, Captain Etienne Boerenveen, the Suriname army's second-in-command, was arrested in Miami, convicted for trafficking cocaine and imprisoned until 1989. As noted earlier, in 1989, General Ochoa Sanchez was one of several officers executed for involvement in trafficking.

In November 1990, Rashleigh Jackson, then the long-standing—twelve years—and respected Foreign Minister of Guyana, was obliged to resign following the indictment of his son Martin, for the possession of drugs. Martin had a previous brush with the law over drugs. In April 1994, Brian and Daren Bernal, sons of Richard Bernal, Jamaica's Ambassador to the United States and the Organization of American States, were arrested at the Norman Manley International Airport in Jamaica and charged with drug trafficking. They had 46 kilos of compressed marijuana in ninety-six cans of what was purported to be Grace pineapple juice, and they were about to board a flight to Washington. Following conviction, they were sentenced, in March 1995, to twelve months' imprisonment and fined a total of J $115,000.

Also in the political elite arena, in November 1994, 121 pounds of cocaine were found in the home of two of the sons of the then Deputy Prime Minister of St. Kitts-Nevis, Sidney Morris. Not only were they arrested and charged with trafficking, but they were later implicated in the murder of a third Morris brother, Vincent. The incident led to the resignation of Deputy Prime Minister Morris and a series of events with serious political and security consequences for the twin island state.

Still in the Eastern Caribbean, on May 6, 1995, Ivor Bird, a brother of Antiguan Prime Minister Lester Bird, was charged in Antigua with attempting to smuggle in 22 pounds of cocaine brought from Venezuela the previous day by an accomplice, Marcus Trotman. He was convicted and fined U. S. $74,000, which he promptly paid. The alternative was two years in jail. One 1995 example in the corporate elite area involved Cecil Abrams, a leading Guyanese businessman who was convicted of trafficking, along with his wife and others. The case involved 5,000 pounds of marijuana found in a ship container in Georgetown, awaiting departure to Miami. Abrams also was convicted on weapons and ammunition charges.[53]

People of all ages and of both sexes are involved in trafficking. Old women are sometimes used, since they do not fit the trafficker profile used by law enforcement agencies. But some are caught. In one case, a sixty-three-year-old Honduran-born American citizen was arrested in Guyana with six pounds of cocaine in her underwear. She was about to board a British West Indian Airways (BWIA) flight to New York when one of the packages fell from under her. The woman, Gwendolyn Martínez, a grandmother, later admitted that she had been recruited in Brooklyn for the job. Upon conviction, she was sentenced to ten years in jail.[54] Martinez was one of several "granny mules" arrested during 1993 and 1994 in Guyana and Trinidad.

Even children are used, because their tender age and innocence are often good camouflage. Use also has been made of cadavers, of both adults and children. In the latter respect, a military official cited the 1994 case where a sixteen-month-old dead baby was used to convey cocaine from Kingston, Jamaica, to London, England. An alert air hostess found it unusual that the "child" had not cried or fidgeted once throughout the eight-and-a-half-hour flight, which led to the discovery.[55]

Some trafficking is done on an individual basis, but most of it is based on simple or elaborate organizational structures and networks. Some operations are very sophisticated, using digital encryption devices, high-frequency transmitters, cellular telephones, beepers, radar tracking devices, flares and sensors for air drops, and other equipment. Some operators are trained in armed combat, counternarcotics surveillance, evasive driving, and other areas. And, of course, traffickers are able to buy the services of specialists such as lawyers, pilots, and engineers.

Most of the structures and networks could not exist without the collusion of people in government and private agencies in various positions and at all hierarchical levels; people in shipping companies, customs and immigration agencies, warehouses, police forces, the military, airlines, export and import companies, stores, cruise ships, trucking companies, farms, factories, bus and taxi operations, and so on. Some officials collude through acts of omission: they just fail to perform certain acts, go to certain places, or return to their posts at a certain time. And considering their earnings for "doing little" or "doing nothing," one could appreciate how many people are susceptible to the corruption, especially in places with poor salaries specifically and or economic deprivation generally.

Trafficking does not always involve direct movement of drugs from place of origin to intended destination; often it is done circuitously. For instance, cocaine would go from Colombia to Jamaica, and then to the United States, sometimes with a further stop in the Bahamas; or from Colombia to Venezuela to Guyana to the United Kingdom, or to the United States, sometimes again with intermediary stops in places like Antigua or Trinidad. In May 1995, for instance, officials in the Dominican Republic uncovered a smuggling operation where Colombian cocaine was being shipped to the United States through Spain and the Dominican Republic.[56]

The circuitous routing of drugs often involves "island hopping," which is facilitated by the proximity factor, in this case the closeness of the

Caribbean countries to each other. The "island hopping" is also possible because of two geographical features mentioned earlier: the island character of most countries, which permits entry from scores, sometimes hundreds, of places; and the physical dispersal of territory, in some cases, examples being the Bahamas, the Virgin Islands, and St. Vincent and the Grenadines.

CONCLUSION

Of all of the elements of the geonarcotics matrix, geography is preeminent when it comes to trafficking in the Caribbean. Location is important, but so too are factors of size, island character, and demography. While there is differentiation in trafficking history, patterns, and amounts from place to place, trafficking is undeniably a region-wide phenomenon. It is crucial to note that although seizures allow one to understand the nature and scope of trafficking, seizures only reveal a small part of the trafficking iceberg. Some sources estimate that only between 15 and 25 percent of drugs from and passing through the Caribbean is seized.

The implications of trafficking go beyond merely the consequences of being transit centers, partly because not everything intended to go through the region actually does so. Some of the cocaine and heroin remain both by default and design, as payment for services, for example, in the latter case. Interestingly, the countries with high cocaine addiction are the very ones that are major cocaine trafficking centers. Moreover, there are problems of crime, arms trafficking, and corruption throughout the region.[57] While these latter issues are beyond our purview here, they must at least be mentioned as realities of the Caribbean's geonarcotics milieu, features of the dangerous dynamics of drugs, geography, power, and politics in the region.

NOTES

1. See Ivelaw L. Griffith, "From Cold War Geopolitics to Post-Cold War Geonarcotics," *International Journal*, vol. 49, no. 1 (winter 1993–94), 1–36.

2. Ivelaw L. Griffith, *The Quest for Security in the Caribbean* (Armonk, N.Y.: M. E. Sharpe, 1993), 51.

3. For a discussion of Latin American drug production in global context, see Bruce M. Bagley and William O. Walker, III, eds., *Drug Trafficking in the Americas* (Miami, Fla.: North South Center, University of Miami,

1994), chs. 5–7, 9, 10, 14, 15, 17, 18, 22, and 23; United Nations, *Report of the International Narcotics Control Board for 1995*, E/INCB/1995/1, January 1996, 37–45; and U. S. Department of State, *International Narcotics Control Strategy Report* [hereafter *INCSR*], 1996, 61–158.

4. William Roy Surrett, *The International Narcotics Trade: An Overview of its Dimensions, Production Sources, and Organizations*, CRS Report for Congress 88–643, October 3, 1988, 1.

5. *INCSR*, 1993, 16.

6. Presentation by General Barry McCaffrey, "Lessons of 1994: Prognosis for 1995 and Beyond," at the 1995 Annual Strategy Symposium cosponsored by the Southern Command and the National Defense University, Miami, April 25, 1995.

7. I am grateful to Brig. (Ret.) David Granger of the Guyana Defense Force for the Guyana-Brazil and the Guyana-Venezuela information, and to Ricardo Mario Rodríguez, Minister Counselor at the Venezuelan Mission to the OAS for the Trinidad-Venezuela information, all provided during May 1995.

8. Anthony P. Maingot, "Laundering the Gains of the Drug Trade; Miami and the Caribbean Tax Havens," *Journal of Interamerican Studies and World Affairs* 30 (summer–fall 1988), 168.

9. For a detailed examination, see Government of the Bahamas, *Report of the Commission of Inquiry into the Illegal Use of the Bahamas for the Transshipment of Dangerous Drugs Destined for the United States* (Nassau, the Bahamas, 1984), 9–51; and Government of the Bahamas, Ministry of Foreign Affairs, *Bahamas Narcotics Control Report*, Nassau, the Bahamas, March 1992.

10. *INCSR*, 1995, 160; *INCSR*, 1996, 163.

11. *INCSR*, 1996, 166.

12. *Report of the Commission of Inquiry*, 31.

13. *Ibid.*, 7–8.

14. See Government of the Bahamas, Ministry of National Security, *Summary Report on the Traffic in Narcotic Drugs Affecting the Bahamas in 1990*, Nassau, the Bahamas, March 28, 1991, 13.

15. *INCSR*, 1994, 136.

16. *INCSR*, 1992, 141.

17. The January 1995 seizure is reported in the *INCSR*, 1995, 119; the total 1995 figure comes from the *INCSR*, 1996, 122.

18. Interviews with Rear Admiral Peter Brady, Chief of Staff, Lt. Col. Allan Douglas, Staff Officer (Operations and Training), and Captain Desmond Edwards, Military Intelligence Officer, JDF Head Quarters, Up Park Camp, Jamaica, December 19, 1994.

19. "Major Ganja Find in Manchester," *Gleaner* (Jamaica), March 8, 1995, 3A.

20. Janice Griffith, "$6M Ganja Haul," *Sunday Sun* (Barbados), 5 July 1992, 1; "Trinidad and Tobago Police Make Big Cocaine Seizure," *Stabroek News* (Guyana), 29 July 1992, 7; "Cops in US $12M Cocaine Timehri Haul," *Stabroek News*, 12 Sept. 1992, 1; "St. Vincent Top Cop Wants Legal Loopholes Tightened," *Caribbean Daylight* (US), 24 Jan. 1993, 16; UNDCP, *Subregional Program Framework for the Caribbean 1994–1995*, Bridgetown, Barbados, Oct. 1994, 8; *INCSR*, 1995, 194–98; and *INCSR*, 1996, 201.

21. Paul Sutton and Anthony Payne, "The Off-limits Caribbean: The United States and the European Dependent Territories," *Annals of the American Academy of Political and Social Sciences*, vol. 533 (May 1994), 92.

22. Sherrie Ann de Leon and Ria Taitt, "T&T Biggest Drug Haul Seized at Sea," *Sunday Express* (Trinidad and Tobago), June 12, 1994, 3; Robert Alonzo, "Third Antiguan Charged with Trafficking in 'Coke'", *Trinidad Guardian* (June 14, 1994), 1; *INCSR*, 1996, 195.

23. See Kenneth Anderson, "$10m Coke Haul off St. Thomas," *St Croix Avis* (USVI), August 27, 1994, 3, 23; Daniel Hierso, "Two Bodies found in St. Martin," *Daily News* (USVI), November 2, 1994, 7; "Marijuana Floating off Caymans," *New York Newsday* (January 5, 1995), 13; and *INCSR*, 1995, 199–201.

24. "British Ship Makes Cocaine Haul," *New York Carib News* (February 3, 1996), 4.

25. *INCSR*, 1996, 209.

26. *INCSR*, 1996, 187.

27. See Rachel Ehrenfeld, "Narco-terrorism and the Cuban Connection," *Strategic Review*, 16 (summer 1988), 58; and Scott B. MacDonald, *Dancing on a Volcano* (New York: Praeger, 1988), 135–36.

28. Andres Oppenheimer, *Castro's Final Hour* (New York: Simon and Schuster, 1992), 41.

29. *Ibid*, 115.

30. Oppenheimer, *Castro's Final Hour*, 127.

31. See Jeff Leen, "Traffickers Tie Castro to Drug Run," *Miami Herald* (July 25, 1996), 1A, 14A; and "Cuba Not Trafficking in Drugs—Havana Official," *Gleaner* (Jamaica), August 12, 1996, A6.

32. "Cocaine Found on Coast Brings 29 to Court," *Miami Herald* (April 14, 1992), 13K.

33. *INCSR*, 1995, 166.

34. This interview is reported in Rensselaer W. Lee, III, "Drugs: The Cuba Connection," *Current History*, vol. 95, (February 1996), 57.

35. *INCSR*, 1994, 184, 185; *INCSR*, 1995, 168–69; and *INCSR*, 1996, 170–71.

36. See U. S. Congress, Senate Committee on Foreign Relations, *Drugs, Law Enforcement, and Foreign Policy: The Cartel, Haiti, and Central*

America. Hearings, Part 4. 100th Congress, 2nd Sess., July 11, 12, and 14, 1988; and Alexandra Marks, "Haiti's Military May Dig in Heels to Keep Lucrative Drug Trade," *Christian Science Monitor,* November 1, 1993, 1, 14.

37. Tim Weiner, "Colombian Drug Trafficker Implicates Haiti Police Chief," *New York Times* (April 22, 1994), A7.

38. *INCSR,* 1995, 176.

39. *INCSR,* 1996, 177.

40. Interview with Winston Felix, Assistant Commissioner of Police (Crime), Eve Leary Police Head Quarters, Georgetown, Guyana, June 30, 1994.

41. See Mohamed Khan, "Drugs Dropped by Mysterious Aircraft," *Stabroek News* (June 8, 1993), 1, 11; and "23 Held in Air-dropped Cocaine Probe," *Stabroek News* (June 9, 1993), 1, 11.

42. *INCSR,* 1995, 174.

43. See *INCSR,* 1994, 189; Alim Hassim, "Marijuana Container valued at US2M," *Stabroek News* (January 6, 1995), 1; and "Three Charged for Trafficking," *Stabroek News* (January 16, 1995), 1, 24.

44. Interview with Lt. Col. Edward Collins, Chief of Military Intelligence, Guyana Defense Force, Camp Ayanganna, June 30, 1994.

45. See "Illegal Airstrip Case: Three Colombians, One Guyanese Charged," *Guyana Chronicle* (January 29, 1989), 1, 4.

46. See Anand Persaud, "117 Pounds of Cocaine Found on GAC Plane," *Stabroek News* (March 18, 1993), 1, 2; and "GAC Offering G1M Reward for Cocaine find Leads," *Stabroek News* (March 19, 1993), 1.

47. Interviews with, among other officials, Brig. Joe Singh, Chief of Staff, Guyana Defense Force, Camp Ayanganna, Georgetown, June 30, 1994; Lt. Cmdr. Gary Best, Acting Commander, Guyana Coast Guard, Coast Guard Headquarters, Georgetown, July 1, 1994; Jules Bernard, Commissioner of Police, Trinidad, Police Headquarters, Port of Spain, July 8, 1994; Orville Durant, Commissioner of Police, Barbados, Police Headquarters, Bridgetown, July 19, 1994; Rear Adm. Peter Brady of the JDF; Supt. Reginald Ferguson, Head of Drug Enforcement Unit, Bahamas Police Force, Nassau, December 22, 1994; and Alvin Goodwin, Deputy Commissioner of Police, Antigua-Barbuda, in Port of Spain, Trinidad, January 21, 1995.

48. Evelyn Larrubia, "Man Charged with Smuggling Cocaine in Stomach," *Fort Lauderdale Sun Sentinel* (March 6, 1996), 1B.

49. Jessica Spart, "The New Drug Mules," *New York Times Magazine* (June 11, 1995), 44–45.

50. Sharon Earle and McPherse Thompson, "Cops Say Visitors Overdosed," *Gleaner* (March 23, 1994); and Margaret Morris, "Cocaine Knocking Tourists out West," *Gleaner* (March 24, 1994).

51. *INCSR*, 1995, 192.

52. See Tony Best, "Cupid's Arrow May Do More Than Pierce the Heart," *New York Carib News* (March 7, 1995), 6.

53. Griffith, *The Quest for Security in the Caribbean*, 229; Lloyd Williams, "Envoy's Son Testifies He Unknowingly Smuggled Drugs to US," *St. Croix Avis* (November 4, 1994); "Drug Scandal Rocks St. Kitts," *St. Croix Avis* (November 26, 1994); Wendella Davidson, "Businessman Abrams Convicted on Illegal Ammunition Charges," *Guyana Chronicle* (February 1, 1995), 7; "Antigua," *Miami Herald* (May 8, 1995), 7A; "Antigua," *Miami Herald* (May 18, 1995), 12A; and telephone interview with Glen Andrade, Director of Public Prosecutions, Jamaica, on April 7, 1995, in relation to the sentences for the Bernal brothers.

54. "10 Years in Jail for Honduran," *Stabroek News* (November 1, 1993), 1.

55. Interview with Captain Edwards of the JDF, December 19, 1994.

56. See "Drugs Going to U. S., Coming from Spain," *Dutch Caribbean Gazette* (Curaçao), (May 24, 1995), 9.

57. For more on these subjects, see Ron Sanders, "Narcotics, Corruption, and Development: The Problems of the Smaller Islands," *Caribbean Affairs*, vol. 30, no. 1 (January–March 1990), 79–92; Louis Blom-Cooper, *Guns for Antigua* (London: Duckworth, 1990); Anthony P. Maingot, *The United States and the Caribbean* (Boulder: Westview, 1994), ch. 7; and Ivelaw L. Griffith, "Caribbean Manifestations of the Narcotics Phenomenon," in Jorge Rodríguez Beruff and Humberto García Muñiz, eds., *Security Problems and Policies in the Post-Cold War Caribbean* (London: Macmillan, 1996), ch. 10.

7

SECURITY IN THE GREATER CARIBBEAN

What Role for Collective Security Mechanisms?

RICHARD J. BLOOMFIELD

> We can safely predict that, regardless of who is president,
> sometime in the next ten years the United States will in-
> tervene once again in the Caribbean.
> —Elliot Abrams[1]

In the decade of the 1990s, the national security discourse in the Greater
Caribbean[2] has radically changed. The strategic and ideological conflicts
that were dominant during the previous decades have given way to a
broad array of problems of a social nature. Depending on one's geographic
location, interests, and prejudices, the new security threat roster may
include drug trafficking and crime, illegal immigration, refugees, the destruction of the environment, destabilizing international capital movements, and the loss of jobs due to the universal trend toward open
markets. This transformation of the security debate obeys two fundamental changes in the international situation: the end of the Cold War and the
economic and psychological effects of the technological revolution.

The end of the Cold War removed the major security concern of the
United States in the region—the possibility of the rise to power of left-
wing, anti-American regimes allied to the Soviet Union. The demise of the
Soviet Union and the fall of communism was accompanied by and/or
contributed to the ending of the civil wars in Central America, thereby

greatly enhancing the internal security of those states and their neighbors. The end of the Cold War also removed what had been a major cause of outside intervention in their internal affairs.

At the same time, rapid technological advances were leading to the integration of the production process across national borders and the spread of information and ideas on a global scale. The result has been to notably increase the permeability of all countries to outside forces. This, in turn, has created a sense of insecurity in societies, like that of the United States, that formerly considered themselves relatively autonomous, and has heightened the insecurity of those that have always been vulnerable to the outside world. It can be said that "globalization" has had the leveling effect of putting the United States in a similar situation of vulnerability to external forces that has long characterized the rest of the Greater Caribbean. Without the Cold War to claim pride of place as the security threat, external challenges that were formerly considered lower order problems of interdependence have been raised in the minds of many Americans to the level of threats to national security.

The fact that these problems do not fit the traditional concept of security threats is not in itself a justification for denying them that status. However, the consequences of the new definition are not merely semantic. The filter through which we perceive problems has much to do with how we structure solutions to them. In the case of the new security agenda, the use of the security-threat paradigm may lead to inappropriate policies.

In the past, security threats have been seen as arising from the aggressive intentions of one state or group of states against another state or group of states and as driven by territorial ambitions or ideological conflict or both. Examples are the wars leading to the creation of the greater German state in the mid-nineteenth century, the two world wars of this century, and, the most recent example, the Gulf War. In contrast, the new security threats are, as often as not, the results of decisions taken by non-state actors, the threatening activities are transnational, that is, they cross borders but may be difficult for the state to control, and their origins are eminently domestic.[3] These characteristics raise the question of whether traditional collective security mechanisms are the appropriate way to deal with them.

COLLECTIVE SECURITY MECHANISMS AND THE NEW THREATS

The defining characteristics of collective security mechanisms is that they are composed of a group of states that perceive a common threat to their security and rely on coercion to deal with the threat. The coercion may take the form of political and economic sanctions or the ultimate sanction, the use of military force.

The two existing collective security mechanisms to which the countries of the Greater Caribbean belong are the United Nations and the Organization of American States, acting under the mandate of the Inter-American Treaty of Reciprocal Assistance (the "Rio Treaty"). Both mechanisms envisage the triggering of a collective security action in the event of a threat to international peace and security, either by the Security Council, in the case of the United Nations, or the Organ of Consultation, in the case of the Rio Treaty. The drafters of the UN Charter (1945) and those of the Rio Treaty (1947) were primarily concerned with conflict between states. The relevant articles in both documents are replete with such terms as "aggression," "armed attack," "territorial integrity," and "common defense."

To be sure, both documents also contain language that could be (and has been) construed to contemplate action in the event of developments other than armed aggression by state against state. The UN Security Council has taken the position that intrastate conflict can threaten international security, and Article 6 of the Rio Treaty refers to "an act of aggression that is not an armed attack . . . or any other fact or situation that might endanger the peace of America" as reasons for the application of the collective security measures embodied in the treaty. The problem, however, is not treaty language but rather, as Richard Ullman has pointed out, "agreement upon what constitutes danger and a shared willingness to use military power to resist a major challenge to the status quo."[4]

The history of the OAS is a case in point. Shortly after the signing of the Rio Treaty and the OAS Charter, the treaty's most powerful member, the United States, became convinced that the major security threat to the Western Hemisphere was not a direct armed intervention by the Soviet Union but rather the installation in one of the American republics of a regime friendly to the Soviet Union. In the years that followed, the U. S. response to political movements that looked to the Soviet Union for support or seemed to be headed in that direction was to try to prevent them from coming to power, or, if they succeeded in doing so, to overthrow them. The problem was that the other members of the OAS often did not regard radical movements or governments as, in themselves, a threat to their security and, in those few cases where they did, the cure offered by the United States—armed intervention—appeared worse than the disease.

These conflicting interpretations presented themselves within a few years of the signing of the Rio Pact because of events in Guatemala. Some officials in the Truman administration regarded the Arbenz government in that country as being under the influence of communists, and intervention was considered but rejected as endangering solidarity with the Latin

American states. The Eisenhower administration had no such compunctions, however. Although Secretary of State John Foster Dulles set the stage for the subsequent U. S.-backed coup against Arbenz by obtaining from a reluctant OAS a resolution stating that "the domination or control of the political institutions of any American State by the international Communist movement" would endanger the security of the hemisphere, the episode set the OAS on a path of increasing internal dissonance and irrelevance that marked its trajectory for the next three decades. During this period, Latin America's belief that radical revolutions were primarily caused by internal factors and its devotion to the nonintervention principle prevented the use of the region's collective security mechanism to thwart the intrusion of a presumably hostile extracontinental power like the Soviet Union into the Hemisphere. What might be expected of a collective security regime created to deal with, say, drug trafficking? The question answers itself.

In addition to questions of principle, there is a practical problem with attempting to use traditional collective security measures to deal with the new types of "security threats." The problem is that efforts to remove such threats must deal with their domestic origins. The government of the country from which the threat emanates must be persuaded to take measures designed to eliminate the source of the threat, which usually is a product of social or economic forces. A collective security organization would not be needed if the government of the source country were already willing to take such measures; recourse to a collective security organization means that the "source" government is recalcitrant, and an implied threat of sanctions is needed to bring it into line.

The difficulty of using such tactics is obvious. For example, the United States' attempts by economic and political pressure to induce the cocaine-producing countries to eradicate coca crops and apprehend and extradite drug dealers. However, this may provoke an intolerable dilemma for the government of the producing country, as is the case in Bolivia, where large numbers of peasants who depend on coca cultivation for their livelihood have mobilized politically against government eradication programs. To take another example, in Colombia in the 1980s, the Medellín drug kingpins reacted to the threat of extradition to the United States with terrorist attacks against government officials and the general public. After hundreds of innocent people were killed, Colombians approved a constitutional amendment prohibiting extradition.

Nevertheless, apparently convinced that the application of outside pressure, if great enough, will force governments to do its bidding, the United States persists in a policy that is a manifest failure, if measured by the only criterion that counts, the availability of cocaine on the street at prices that U. S. consumers are willing to pay. Would collective coercion be any more effective in overcoming these obstacles than unilateral coercion has been? Could a multilateral body be expected to sit in formal judgment on whether country X is doing enough to deal with the drug problem or the environment? Moreover, would the members of such an organization, most of whom have "intermestic" problems of their own, be in favor of using sanctions in such cases? Defining problems like the drug trade, the environment, and migration flows as "security" problems can be a source of confusion, or worse, if it leads to attempts to solve the problems by the use of collective security mechanisms that are, by definition, unsuited for that task.

This is not to say that these problems do not warrant or are not susceptible to cooperative measures among states. Quite the contrary, they are the kind of issues that are the result of the growing interdependence of societies on this planet and that cry out for international cooperation for their resolution. Closer cooperation at the subregional level is essential to address the challenges like crime, drugs, and unemployment in the small states of the Greater Caribbean, which in turn, can be the source of similar problems elsewhere in the area, including the United States. Some of this cooperation may take the form of subregional international regimes. But while all collective security mechanisms are international regimes, all international regimes are not collective security mechanisms, and it behooves us to take care not to conflate the two.

THE ROLE OF COLLECTIVE SECURITY IN THE GREATER CARIBBEAN

Are we to conclude that there is no role for collective security mechanisms in the solution to the kinds of transnational problems that are now confronting the Greater Caribbean? Not entirely. There is one issue that is an appropriate candidate for the use of collective security measures: threats to democracy. Paradoxically, this is the most "domestic" issue of them all, for it goes to the heart of sovereignty—who is to rule. That same characteristic, however, is what makes a threat to democracy more like a classic security threat: democracy, by making the entire people of a state the rulers, is the ultimate expression of sovereignty.

This ideal is presumably what prompted the members of the OAS to state in the organization's charter that democracy was essential to their well-being and the fulfillment of their "high aims."[5] The problem, of course, was that, at the insistence of the Latin Americans, the same charter enshrined the nonintervention principle,[6] which was understandable, given the proclivity of the United States to intervene in their affairs during the previous fifty years. It took almost another half century, and the brutal authoritarian regimes that had swept over Latin America in the 1960s and 1970s, for the Latin Americans to decide that democracy had to be accorded the same prominence as nonintervention and that some compromise of the latter had to be accepted as the price of defending the former. In 1991, the OAS made the momentous decision that the protection of democratic institutions is a legitimate function of collective action, including economic and political sanctions (but not the use of armed force.)

In addition to the general arguments in favor of democracy as a collective security interest, there is a practical one: authoritarian regimes are often the root causes of the sorts of transnational problems that are now seen as threatening the general welfare, as, for example, refugees, or are themselves part of the problem, as in the case of drug trafficking. Moreover, dictatorships are likely to be intransigent in the face of international pressure to remedy the situation, since the cure could spell their own downfall.

The rudiments of an inter-American regime to defend democracy already exist. The catalyst for this nascent regime was provided by Resolution 1080, approved by the OAS General Assembly at its annual meeting in 1991. In what has come to be known as the Santiago Commitment, Resolution 1080 provides that, in the event of "any sudden or irregular interruption of the democratic institutional process or of the legitimate exercise of power by the democratically elected government in any of the Organization's member states" an emergency meeting of OAS foreign ministers will be convoked within ten days to decide on a collective reaction. While the resolution does not require more than that the foreign ministers "adopt any decisions deemed appropriate," in fact in the four coup situations that followed the Santiago meeting, the foreign ministers have shown a surprising willingness to go beyond mere rhetoric in order to protect democracy. In each case, they have not only condemned the overthrow as illegal and called for a prompt return to democratic rule, but they have resorted to economic and political sanctions to back up their demands.[7]

Resolution 1080, the precedents set by the four "test" cases, and a subsequent amendment to the charter that suspends any member in which a democratically elected government has been replaced by force, have begun the process of building an inter-American defense-of-democracy regime.

Yet many Latin American states have mixed feelings about a regime to protect democracy. They are wary of a precedent that enlarges the jurisdiction of international organizations to cover what traditionally has been considered a domestic matter. Some governments feel vulnerable about drug enforcement, others about environmental degradation, others on the issue of human rights. They are particularly fearful of attempts to define these and other traditionally domestic problems as "security" issues, lest it increase outside interference in their affairs. For these reasons, most Latin American countries do not want a defense-of-democracy regime that is too strong, that is, one with the power to use force.[8]

This poses a particular problem for the small states of the Caribbean Basin. The majority do not have the economic resources to allay the kind of popular discontent that can weaken respect for democracy and, in some, democratic institutions do not have deep roots. In several, there are ethnic divisions that can undermine even long-standing democratic institutions. Some of these small democracies would be hard put to defend against an attack by a ruthless, intransigent cabal like the one that ousted President Aristide in 1991. Some are obvious prey to corruption by international criminal gangs, whose financial resources are greater than the GNP of many of these states. Some are susceptible to the demagoguery of politicians aspiring to rule behind a facade of democracy. In most of Central America, there is currently an uneasy modus vivendi between the armed forces and the civilian authorities, with the military resisting efforts by the government to reduce its considerable autonomy, especially in matters that affect its corporate interests. In short, without an outside guarantor of their integrity, democracies in many of these small states may ultimately fail.

THE CASE FOR SUBREGIONAL COLLECTIVE SECURITY REGIMES

But why single out the small states of the region, when democracy in some of the larger states is facing similar threats? Is that not espousing a double standard? The answer is yes, and with good reason.

U. S. presidents see themselves as actors on the world stage, by which they mean Europe and Asia. In reality, their most difficult—and unwanted—roles are often in what they regard as a sideshow, the Caribbean Basin. Given that most of the security crises in the Caribbean have occurred in the area's small states, U. S. presidents have often been tempted to deal with the latest distraction in the hinterland by taking swift and decisive action—to send in the marines. That has been the pattern of U.S. interventions in the Western Hemisphere. Of the seventeen U. S. presidents who have thus far held office in this century, twelve have seriously contemplated, threatened, or resorted to unilateral military intervention in the Caribbean Basin.[9]

As evidenced by the 1989 invasion of Panama and the 1994 occupation of Haiti, situations that can lead to intervention did not end with the cold war. On the contrary, transnational forces like illegal immigration, refugees, the drug trade, human rights activists, and ethnic groups with ties to the Basin have increased the pressure on U. S. presidents to become entangled in the affairs of the region. Such problems used to be lumped under the term "low" politics (as distinguished from the "high" politics of relations among the Great Powers), but it is their mundane nature that makes them politically explosive domestically. They hit society where it lives; they affect how people vote. Immigration and refugees are hot-button political issues in Florida and California. The narcotics trade is a hot-button issue everywhere, not just because of its deleterious effects on public health, but because it is intimately associated with the violence that plagues society today. Thanks to lobbying by well-organized and vociferous nongovernmental organizations like Americas Watch and Amnesty International, nations have been forced to pay more than lip service to the human rights provisions in the UN Declaration on Human Rights.

All this is the result of societies interacting directly with one another unmediated by governments. Ronald Reagan's policy toward Nicaragua was a hotly debated issue, but mainly among intellectuals and the foreign policy elites. The general public had views on the matter—largely opposing—but it was not a burning issue for the average man in the street whose sons and daughters were not dying in the contra war. In contrast, whether illegal immigrants are entitled to tax-supported social services and free education is a vital issue for everyone in places like California, and presidents, senators, and governors must pay attention. To paraphrase Tip O'Neill's[10] maxim, that "all politics is local," much of foreign policy is now domestic politics.

The longer such inflammatory issues engage the U. S. public and the longer diplomacy fails to produce solutions, the closer U. S. political leaders come to see punitive action and coercion as the appropriate response. This is the rationale of recent federal and state legislation to deny legal and illegal immigrants and their children social services. It is at the heart of our "supply-side" drug policy.

In extreme cases, where the problem is seen as being generated by a uncooperative foreign government, a president may be tempted by the idea of military intervention if the cost of doing so is not high, that is, if the offending regime is not capable of effective resistance, which is the case in the small Caribbean states. As noted, this is most likely to be the case when the government is in the hands of usurpers of the democratic order. In the last several years, however, it has become excruciatingly difficult for U. S. presidents to practice unilateral intervention. That is all to the good if it inhibits them from making the mistakes of the past. The Vietnam syndrome is not necessarily a bad thing, but it can be if it leaves a U. S. president with no alternative to deal with a situation that is both the source of a serious domestic U. S. social problem and the cause of the destruction of democratic institutions in a hemisphere that has declared them essential.

This is the dilemma Bill Clinton faced in Haiti. One can argue about the president's motives for wanting to get rid of the Cedras regime. Surely one of the driving forces behind his determination was the domestic political problem presented by the influx of Haitian refugees: they would not have been coming in the numbers they did if Haiti had had a democratic government. It is not hard to imagine parallel situations arising in the future. It is doubtful, however, that a U. S. president will always be able to count on the last-minute intervention of a Jimmy Carter and the backing of the UN Security Council.

What U. S. presidents need is a multilateral collective security regime for the defense of democracy in the Basin that will deter attempts to overthrow democracy and provide legitimacy for U. S. participation in a collective intervention to restore it, if that becomes necessary

There will be those who denounce this proposal as a cover for the United States to practice intervention at will. Yet the absence of such a regime has not deterred the United States in the past. A regime would have more of a restraining influence than no regime. For one, interventions have become unpopular with the U. S. public, and one directed at a democracy would be even more so. It also is unlikely that the members of a Caribbean defense-of-democracy regime would vote in favor of an intervention in such circumstances. The regime would thus reinforce the inhibiting effect on a president who was contemplating a foreign expedition that was already opposed by the majority of voters.

FROM THE PERSPECTIVE OF THE SMALL STATES
OF THE CARIBBEAN BASIN

The history of many small states in the Caribbean Basin has shown that their security is directly related to the degree of democracy enjoyed by each. They have a powerful collective stake in a strong defense-of-democracy regime: the overthrow of democracy in one of their number almost inevitably leads to the insecurity of the rest. Authoritarian rule tends to lead to internal conflict or a breakdown of law and order that typically spills over borders and provokes external intervention by near neighbors or the United States, or both. In addition, without strong democratic institutions, these states are less likely to be able to meet what are ultimately the threats to their security: the challenges posed by economic globalization. Without a sense of participation in the process of decision making, their citizens are unlikely to be willing to make the changes and sacrifices that will be necessary to become self-reliant in a world in which foreign aid and protective trading arrangements are shrinking.[11]

The small states of the Greater Caribbean must rely heavily on outside powers to come to their aid if their democratic institutions are attacked. The best way to harness the power of outsiders on behalf of their fragile democracies—and to exercise some control over it—would be to create their own collective defense-of-democracy regimes.

These small states and the United States now have a strong common interest in a subregional defense-of-democracy regime in the Caribbean Basin.

WHAT KIND OF COLLECTIVE SECURITY REGIME?

Defense-of-democracy regimes at the subregional level would establish norms, spell out a series of sanctions that could be invoked should a member violate the norms, and take the initiative to seek assistance of outsiders like the UN, the OAS, or a "coalition of the willing" to enforce the sanctions. It would define the terms of reference for other international assistance and provide legitimacy to outside involvement in their internal affairs. By making it clear in advance that those who seized power by force would be isolated and punished, the regimes would act as a deterrent to those contemplating coups or other subversions of democracy.

Institutional frameworks for such regimes already exist in the two groups of small states in the Caribbean Basin, the Caribbean Community, and the Organization of Central American States. In neither case, however, have these organizations taken steps toward a defense-of-democracy regime.

To be sure, long-standing suspicions and rivalries among the small states of the Basin are an obstacle to their creation. Nevertheless, there is a successful precedent. The Esquipulas Agreement, signed by the five Central American presidents on August 7, 1987, and follow-on agreements became the instrument by which the Central Americans took the peace process out of the hands of external actors like the United States and the Contadora countries and fashioned their own solution, one based on the principle that ideological differences should be settled by free elections, not at the barrel of a gun. The principles established at Esquipulas permitted the Central Americans to decide what kind of outside intervention they wanted—and provided legitimacy to various OAS and UN commissions for repatriation of refugees, disarmament of the combatants, the monitoring of elections, and further outside mediation, such as the UN-sponsored peace talks in both El Salvador and Guatemala.

Unfortunately, the Esquipulas framework seems to have been ephemeral. While its principal architects, former Presidents Oscar Arias of Costa

Rica and Vinicio Cerezo of Guatemala, believe the agreements are still in effect,[12] it is doubtful that their view is shared widely by most Central Americans, who seem to look upon them as having been an *ad hoc* solution—a part of history.

As for the Caribbean community, it too has not brought itself to dealing with the collective defense of democratic institutions, which perhaps reflects a complacency brought on by the deeper roots of democracy in the English-speaking Caribbean.

Yet this is not the time for complacency. The Haiti crisis demonstrated the inadequacy of existing arrangements. As a result, the idea of subregional efforts to provide security and protect democracy should have greater credence. One hopeful sign was the willingness of a number of Anglophone states in the region to participate in the Haiti intervention in a policing role.

CONCLUSION

At the heart of the difficulty of creating a world order based on international cooperation to promote humane values is the tension between national sovereignty and the need for effective collective action. The degree to which sovereignty is traded for the benefits of international cooperation will vary greatly from one region of the world to the other. One scholar believes that the process is dependent on the spread of "complex interdependence," which is, not by accident, a characteristic of pluralistic democracies.

The small states of the Caribbean Basin are, by force of geography if nothing else, being drawn into the complex interdependence of the North American continent. They have chosen democratic forms of government, which are essential if they are to succeed in adapting to the demands of interdependence. The proposed subregional security regimes are a way by which these small states can better cope with the challenges of adaptation. By creating collective security systems of their own that would allow them to mobilize international support in defense of their democratic institutions, they would enhance their security as well as preserve a measure of control over the process.

The increasing interpenetration of the societies of the United States and those of the rest of the Basin means that continuing U. S. involvement in the affairs of those countries is inevitable. The proposal for small-state regimes in the Caribbean Basin for the defense of democracy seeks to find a way that such involvement can be a positive force for the region's future, while avoiding the discredited patterns of the past.

NOTES

1. In his remarks at a conference on "International Security in the Greater Caribbean," held at the Center for International Affairs, Harvard University, October 20, 1995.

2. I take the "Greater Caribbean" to be the same area as what has come to be called the Caribbean Basin, that is, all of the countries the shores of which are washed by the Caribbean Sea. In this chapter, the terms are used interchangeably. As will become apparent, my particular concern is with the twenty-two small states of the Basin, defined as those having populations of 10 million or less.

3. Hence, the name "intermestic," coined by Abraham Lowenthal.

4. Richard Ullman, "Enlarging the Zone of Peace," *Foreign Policy* 80 (fall 1990), 112.

5. Charter of the OAS, Prologue and Article 3 (d).

6. Charter of the OAS, Articles 18–22.

7. The four cases are the overthrow of President Aristide of Haiti in 1991, the autogolpe (self-coup) by President Alberto Fujimori in Peru in 1992, the aborted autogolpe by President Jorge Serrano of Guatemala in 1993, and the aborted coup attempt by some Paraguayan military in 1996.

8. Richard J. Bloomfield, "Making the Western Hemisphere Safe for Democracy? The OAS Defense-of-Democracy Regime," *Washington Quarterly*, vol. 17, no. 2 (spring 1994).

9. By my reckoning, the exceptions are Harding, Hoover, Nixon, Ford, and Carter. Carter did propose the intervention of an Interamerican Peace Force in the Nicaraguan civil war.

10. Thomas P. O'Neill, Democratic Congressman from Massachusetts (1952–1986) and Speaker of the House of Representatives (1976–1986.) (It has been pointed out to me that today's college sophomores probably have never heard of Tip O'Neill.)

11. Robert A. Pastor and Richad D. Fletcher, "Twenty-first Century Challenges for the Caribbean and the United States: Toward a New Horizon," Jorge I. Domínguez, Robert A. Pastor, and Delisle Worrell, eds., *Democracy in the Caribbean: Political, Economic, and Social Perspectives* (Baltimore: Johns Hopkins University Press, 1993); and Jorge I. Domínguez, "The Caribbean in a New International Context: Are Freedom and Peace a Threat to its Prosperity?", Anthony Bryan, ed., *The Caribbean: New Dynamics in Trade and Political Economy* (Transaction Press, 1995).

12. Conversations with the author in 1993.

8

New Issues on the Regional Security Agenda for the Caribbean

Drugs, Environment, Migration, and Democratic Stability

INSTITUTO DE ALTOS ESTUDIOS
DE LA DEFENSA NACIONAL,
VENEZUELA

INTRODUCTION

The new world order has set in motion a variety of regional processes, from dissolution to integration. At the same time, individual countries are searching for their place in this new order by following old and new ideological trends that affect their own security as much as that of the superpowers that head each regional geopolitical group. In addition to the breakup of the USSR and the former Yugoslavia in the North, one may observe the fundamentalist power of Islam and the ongoing integration of the South, particularly in Latin America. For their part, the growing industrial poles exercise influence over their own peripheries as a means of expanding their economic capacities and realizing their potential in terms of human and material resources. In this context, security becomes more complex and global. Threats arise in new forms and with different effects. They demand renewed strategic approaches and a revision of the security patterns of the past, perhaps even their replacement by a new collective concept of security.

In addition to the issues mentioned in the title of this chapter, it would be useful to note others that may constitute "threats" to world and regional peace.[1] An exhaustive examination of these topics is beyond the scope of this section, but the topics are at least worth evaluating.

Domestic disturbances prevailing throughout the world, but especially in underdeveloped countries. These could be classified under the generic rubric of "political instability with regional and worldwide impact."

Crime and administrative corruption; violence in general and, specifically, structural violence, which constitutes an obstacle to peace at the domestic level as well as in international relations at the regional level.

Fundamentalism as a sociopolitical phenomenon, whose impact extends beyond the countries that espouse the religious doctrines that give rise to it. Fundamentalism also affects other countries by creating migrations of people in search of a better standard of living or a more promising future.

The continuation of nuclear arms production and the obstacles related to arms limitation, arms reduction and nuclear testing.

The proliferation of weapons of mass destruction, with potentially lethal effects on people in areas exposed to their use. This topic is relevant not only to underdeveloped countries without nuclear capabilities, but also to countries that are more advanced on the technological scale.

Ultranationalist and ultraconservative attitudes, which tend to frustrate cooperation that may promote collective interests. These attitudes threaten to reverse the progress made in the development of national and international criteria for mutual understanding. Such attitudes reverberate throughout the world, especially around issues of world economy, the transfer of sovereignty, and border disputes. They may have historic causes or even valid legal justifications, but they nonetheless reduce the possibility of cooperation and integration for peace in a future regional context.

In *War and Anti-War*, Alvin and Heidi Toffler adopt suggestions from Edward Luttwak, Albert Bergsten, and Lester Turow,[2] that accord primacy to economic over security issues in the current global situation. "Knowledge" continues to be relevant for war- and peacemaking because it is the main factor in the competitive struggle of strategic actors. Human beings (the "Tecnitas," according to Dr. Mayz Vallenilla) are on the verge of becoming computers or data banks as they absorb and are absorbed by the existing cybernetic apparati.[3]

This array of threats affects the new security agenda of the more advanced countries as well as that of the less fortunate ones, such as the Latin American nations. The latter are required to raise their level of strategic capabilities, despite having weak economies, increased debt, and a slow educational process.

REGIONAL SECURITY

The term "Architecture of Regional Security" calls attention to populations, their relationships, and the sociopolitical equilibrium.[4] Regional security is in fact a process of "collective security," whose goal is to reverse the geopolitical lines which, in the past, radiated outward from a given country toward its neighbors or perimeters. The new goal of regional security is to convert geopolitical lines into regional vectors that link the common interests of the region.[5] As a consequence, countries are channeling their efforts into processes of integration by following the model of old Europe, which after a thousand years of conflict has nearly succeeded in securing integration. We hope the same is achieved in Latin America and the Caribbean, where there is an ongoing effort to reduce the destabilizing effects of the region's uncertain historical evolution. We also hope to replace these effects with a regional integrationist arrangement in which economic forces are unified for the sake of the collective good, as in the Latin American Economic System (SELA), the Latin American Association for Integration (ALADI), the Andean Pact, MERCOSUR, CARICOM, the Rio Group, the Association of Caribbean States, the Regional Security System of the Caribbean (RSS), and a global architecture provided by NAFTA and the permanent presence of the United States, the main pillar of hemispheric security.

Integration and cooperation are replacing bilateralism throughout the hemisphere. The result is the creation of new, collectively oriented tendencies. The Miami Summit and other meetings, along with studies aimed at promoting measures of mutual trust in the southern part of the continent, serve to reinforce this new development. As Ivelaw Griffith noted:

> The processes of continuity and change are part of the new problems of regional security. Vulnerability still exists as a general concern, but dynamic transformations at the global and regional

level make geopolitics no longer a factor of great concern. Likewise, intervention is not a priority, notwithstanding the situation in Haiti. Democratizing tendencies are spreading across the region, and the militarization of the region is not a main concern these days.[6]

THE CONCEPT OF SECURITY AT THE CURRENT JUNCTURE

The famous (or infamous) "National Security Doctrine" has been widely eclipsed in Latin America. Security is currently based on democratic stability, observance of human rights, environmental protection, the promotion of development and peace, collective coexistence, regional integration, the resolution of domestic socioeconomic problems, and the reduction of domestic social conflict.

Peace is directly related to security. The "Lato Sensu" idea of security, popular among intellectuals in developing countries and increasingly plausible even to politicians, traditionalists, and military followers of "realism" or "power politics," has been conceptualized in relation to a set of sociopolitical variables suggested by Johann Galtung and his followers. These variables include, among others, human and social needs, moral values, and democracy. It follows that the study of security and peace requires a thorough inquiry into the persistence of severe inequality and the shortcomings of political administration and leadership that contribute to structural violence, therefore undermine social harmony and collective welfare.

Alberto Muller Rojas, a professor in the Department of Administrative, Juridical, and Political Sciences at the University of Caracas, Venezuela, argues that "the countries of the Caribbean region have realized that neither by themselves nor jointly can they face threats from Europe, Asia, or North America. In adopting a broad perspective for promoting peace, which includes not only military but also political and economic measures, they have found the most adequate way to promote trust. Therefore, they have agreed to develop hemispheric and regional institutions with U. S. participation that might minimize the capacity of outsiders to intervene or threaten them."[7]

As this suggests, the definition of security has been gradually approximating the definition of peace. By defining security in terms of social welfare or the realization of citizens' aspirations and interests, security is seen to be directly related to peace. The latter becomes the ultimate end of the former, once mutual understanding and cooperation have been reached through cultural and educational advancement.[8]

It is possible that the Association of Caribbean States, which came about as a result of recommendations made by the heads of government of CARICOM, will permit common development and become a new collective instrument for the affirmation of a Caribbean identity, as well as strengthening Caribbean nations in dealings with countries outside of the Basin. The first meeting of government officials and representatives of the Association of Caribbean States, held in the Port of Spain in August 1995, resolved to "continue to promote the process of respect for the sovereignty and integrity of the countries of the area, their rights and self-determination, as well as democratic principles, human rights, and the peaceful resolution of conflicts." But the most important proposal was a plan of action outlined in the same declaration.

DRUGS, DRUG TRAFFICKING, AND SECURITY

Drugs are a grave social problem, and their production, sale, and consumption have become an important issue of state security. These activities pose a real threat. According to a recent (February 1995) publication by the U. S. Joint Chiefs of Staff, one strategy for facing this threat could be regional, with one vertex in the United States, the chief drug-consuming country par excellence, and the other vertices in the drug-producing countries, drug-bridge countries, and the countries that serve as financial centers, sheltering the operating funds as well as "laundered" funds.[9]

To respond regionally to the drug threat requires making strategic activities more cohesive and facilitating cooperation among the operating units conducting this war in each country. But the armed forces that have adopted this task as part of their operational missions are taking on a delicate commitment, because activities related to drug trafficking have a dangerous proclivity for generating corruption. There is a need for some structure capable of resisting this proclivity.[10]

This is, of course, a simplified account of the war against drugs. This war has been going on for years and remains in a permanent state of fluctuation throughout an area of millions of square kilometers.

In Latin America and the Caribbean, we are convinced that the military strategy of the U. S. takes this threat into account. We are also convinced that the U. S. military recognizes that drug trafficking, like terrorism, is one of its most dangerous adversaries. We hope this will lead them to cooperate with the governmental agencies of the countries in the South by means of technological support and other resources in accordance with the global strategy suggested in this chapter.[11]

MIGRATION AND ITS EFFECTS

We have already mentioned that streams of immigrants are penetrating Europe, generating distress among the local population, producing genuine "mosaics," as Toffler calls them, and creating concerns about security in the countries that are receiving the largest number of them, such as Germany, France, and England. The following remarks are intended to serve as an introduction to the issue of migration in the Caribbean region.

Segments of the population of many Caribbean countries that were colonies until recently have emigrated to their former metropoli. In the 1980s, approximately 266,000 French Antilleans were residing in France. Some 519,000 nationals from the British West Indies were residing in England, and 190,000 Surinam nationals were residing in Holland. More than one million Cubans and 2.7 million Puerto Ricans were living in the United States. The main emigration-generating Caribbean countries are Puerto Rico, Cuba, Haiti, the Dominican Republic, Jamaica, Trinidad and Tobago, Guyana, and Barbados. The principal immigration-receiving countries are the United States, Great Britain, France, Canada, and Holland.[12]

The Caribbean Basin is an active field of social mobility along classic horizontal and vertical lines. Although there are cases of immigrants returning to their homeland, the majority head northward, with an appreciable number (approximately 100,000) also headed toward the Basin countries of Venezuela, Colombia, and Mexico. With regard to vertical mobility, it is interesting to note that the migrant population is adapting to new cultures and acquiring a variety of skills that equip them to work as specialized laborers, whether abroad or within their own country if they return. This means an improvement in the quality of life for at least a small percentage of the population that otherwise would have continued to suffer the adversities endemic to marginalization.

One remaining problem is migration from countries in crisis conditions, that is, refugees. These include the well-known migrations from Cuba and the more recent migrations from Haiti, which have increased by some 500,000 people. In addition, 100,000 Nicaraguans settled in Florida and other states. There are also, of course, a large number of Salvadoran, Guatemalan, Honduran, Mexican, and Colombian immigrants to which we must add for the first time in history a migratory movement of Venezuelans to North America and Europe.[13]

A reexamination of this problem is required to evaluate the effect of migrations on the receiving countries and their counterparts, as well as the favorable or unfavorable effects that growing levels of migration are producing in the various countries of the Caribbean region. It is well known that, by sustaining a regime of control, the United States is intent on keeping an accurate count on migrations. The United States assigns quotas to each country, based on periodically evaluated policies, with the goal of reducing the number of illegal migrants and their socioeconomic impact. However, much has been said about the utilization of these immigrants and their engagement in informal activities, especially in New York, California, and Miami. In this sense, one could speak of a favorable economic balance in the receiving countries. However, one cannot escape thinking about the problems of exploitation, labor relations, discrimination against foreigners, and racial antagonism. These have given rise to genuine local conflicts that will require more effective attention in the future. The Hispanic population in Florida has grown into a sizable conglomerate that deserves greater equality in social care and labor treatment. In the "emigration-generating" countries, the situation is different. Economically, they enjoy a double benefit: the reduction of social responsibility, and a modest inflow of quantities of monetary remittances. These factors somewhat alleviate poverty for many families in these societies.

In sum, harmonizing U. S. policies with the interests and concerns of the people from the poorest and most populated countries of the Caribbean region is a complex task. Taking into account the variables suggested here, and many others beyond the scope of this chapter, would provide a more accurate picture. This in turn would encourage the adoption of policies that might alleviate the pain of both the "exporting" and "receiving" countries.

ENVIRONMENTAL SECURITY

According to a document in progress at IAEDEN, "La Seguridad y la Paz en América Latina" (Security and Peace in Latin America), "The idea of environmental security has been recognized as a precondition of the stability of developing countries. . . . It requires an appropriate level of economic support, popular awareness of the issues, and an efficient national leadership capable of designing and applying the necessary policies. In the underdeveloped world, these conditions are scarce; thus, environmental security requires education and external support in addition to long-term planning, which should necessarily take into account these three levels":[14]

> *Global*: Competition for natural resources, the ozone layer, the loss of biodiversity, the arms race and proliferation of weapons of mass destruction, nuclear and toxic waste from the industrialized world, etc.

Regional: Environmental depredation, regional conflicts over scarce resources, pollution along border regions, and "export" of polluting agents and other factors that affect the region's air, water, and lands.

National: The violation of environmental protection laws, the effects of multipurpose chemical pollutants from industry and agriculture, and the growing of hallucinogenic plants.

When carried out by specialized organizations in each country, such as the official departments of renewable natural resources, activities to counter these problems can generate appropriate solutions. But when carried out by the armed forces or the police, these activities require special attention. In the majority of cases, these forces need advice in applying the prescribed measures.

The Latin American and Caribbean regions are suffering the consequences of environmental deterioration as they previously suffered the indiscriminate exploitation of forests and mineral resources. Today, the countries of these regions are adopting the idea of environmental security in the hope of recovering from the damage already done and of reorienting their policies. Governments as well as specialized segments of the private sector and the armed forces are pooling their capabilities in defense of the environment. At the regional level, too, the most promising approach would be mutual coordination and cooperation that would harmonize national policies, especially along border regions.

Deforestation, for example, which is occurring at an accelerated pace, especially in some Caribbean islands, aggravates levels of poverty and privation and threatens social stability and order. Meteorological events, especially hurricanes, produce another kind of damage that requires foresight and collective action. The disposal of toxic waste, as well as the gradual pollution of the Caribbean Sea, where there is little monitoring, point to the need for joint efforts. Left to their own devices, the countries of this region lack sufficient means to counteract this pollution, which in the long run threatens them all.

We have usually considered security in reference to international conflicts. But there is only one planet; its resources are limited and its atmosphere, land, and waters belong to humanity. The behavior of most countries all too often ignores the real security issues, which go beyond mere individual interests, national objectives, or aspirations for power. World security is fundamentally biological in nature. It entails the survival of life on the planet; making food available to ever-growing populations and preserving a clean and livable environment. This is the best recipe for international security and also for peace.[15]

DEMOCRATIC STABILITY

The political history of the countries of Latin America has been an alternation between dictatorship and democracy. Political stability has been virtually nonexistent. It is only now that stability has been achieved in most countries. However, the ghost of military intervention still lingers. In the Caribbean region, Cuba is a special case, having maintained its system against very intense adverse circumstances and socioeconomic pressures for change. Haiti remains an enigma. The key question is, What will happen after the U. S. troops leave? Haiti is a messianic country and probably too poor to adopt a straightforward liberal democracy, as most of its neighbors have. Jamaica is an example of democratic evolution, like other English-speaking countries of the Caribbean, where British influence has served to sustain parliamentary activity and political stability. The Dominican Republic is developing a process of democratic participation within a tradition of civil-military rule and with an electoral dynamic that is reasonably coherent. Except for Dominica and Grenada, the traditional "golpism" (i.e., propensity to coup d'état) of many Latin American countries has not had much effect among these nations.

This brief description of the principal cases in the Caribbean Basin indicates that there has been some progress since the time when differences between the Caribbean Legion and the tropical dictators of some neighboring countries were aired. The current situation offers hope of further progress through joint programs and cooperation with the United States and Canada and through socioeconomic links with the larger countries in the Basin. In general, it is evident that democratic stability in the region depends on three bulwarks: governability, progress in institutional development, and attitudes toward the relations of the armed forces with the rest of society. And while it is true that some island-countries possess only limited paramilitary forces, these forces are nonetheless indispensable to securing public trust and social order. We believe a subregional security system in the Caribbean can contribute to securing democracy in the area.

Governability in Latin America has been steadily improving. Social problems, political troubles, and economic shortcomings make matters worse, but we are confident these hurdles will be overcome. Governability is more difficult under a democracy than under a dictatorship, and in some situations authoritarianism may seem necessary to achieve order. Indeed, recent trends in some countries regarding the disrepute of political parties and the rise of electoral abstentionism suggest that there is a need for an active educational program and more domestic efforts to promote institutional and civic development in these countries, to forestall a resort to coercive means. In addition, achieving higher levels of democracy in

Latin America and the Caribbean requires a prudent time frame, effective support from the more advanced countries, and an effort toward real regional integration.

CONCLUSION

The new regional security agenda in the Caribbean Basin is rooted in a vision of a peaceful future instead of armed security. The domination that stemmed from regional hegemonies has been succeeded by a movement toward liberal democracy, in which human rights and environmental preservation take their place alongside the eternal struggle for local, national, or regional interests.

There is an old saying: Crises must be left to do their job. In other words, not all crises are wholly bad. This is why we remain optimistic about the region's future possibilities.

NOTES

1. The brochure "Meeting the Challenges of Regional Security" by the Honorable Leonard Sullivan Jr., February 1994, contains an analysis of some of these topics under the name of the U. S. Army War College, Institute of Strategic Studies.

2. See Alvin and Heidi Toffler, *War and Anti-War: Survival at the Dawn of the 21st Century* (New York: Little Brown, 1993), 16, 139.

3. See Ernesto Mayz Vallenilla, *El hombre en el mundo actual*. Conference: Institute of Higher Studies of National Defense, 1975.

4. This expression is explained in a document sent to the Institute of Higher Studies of National Defense by the Venezuelan Military Attaché in Belgium, Colonel Rafael María Estrada.

5. See Carlos E. Celis Noguera, *Geopolítica regional*. Edited by the Secretariat of the Presidency of the Republic, Caracas, 1995.

6. Ivelaw L. Griffith, "Los emergentes desafíos de Seguridad en el Caribe." Synthesis taken from *Paz y seguridad en las Américas*. Florida International University (August 1995), no. 4.

7. General Alberto Muller Rojas, "Los problemas de la seguridad en la región del Caribe: Perspectiva Venezolana." INVESP papers. (July–December 1993), 60.

8. Taken from a work in progress, "La Seguridad y la Paz en América Latina," by General Carlos Celis Noguera, IAEDEN, 1995, 15, 16.

9. See Military Strategy of the U. S. A., the JCS. "National Military Strategy" (February 1995). Translated by IAEDEN. The fight against drugs is part of the mission of the armed forces.

10. See *Geopolítica regional*, op. cit.

11. Rosa de Olmo. "¿Prohibir o domesticar? The politics of drugs in Latin America." This study contains important information about drug movements in the Caribbean and the impact of drugs in Latin America.

12. See "El Caribe y Cuba en la post guerra fría" by Andrés Serbín and Joseph Tulchin. Editorial Nueva Sociedad, INVESP, Caracas 1994, p. 215. The author, Jorge Duany, provides data on the volume of immigrants coming from different countries of the Caribbean and migrations toward the North.

13. The previously cited research study, "Más allá de la válvula de escape: Tendencias recientes en la migración caribeña," by Jorge Duany, presents a detailed analysis of the migrations in the Caribbean in all senses.

14. See SSI, Special Report, "Environmental security," A Department of Defense partnership for peace. Edited by Kent Hughes Butts. U. S. Army War College, 1994.

15. "Seguridad y paz en América Latina," 179, 187.

9

CONCLUSION

MICHAEL C. DESCH

In spite of the end of the Cold War, the Caribbean security environment will remain challenging. Drug lords have replaced pirates and guerillas as the main security problem in the region, but the American Mediterranean continues to be plagued not only by natural but also by such man-made calamities as economic dislocation, environmental degradation, social instability, and political conflict. The Caribbean was a major locus of security competition during the Cold War,[1] and as the chapters in this book suggest, it will remain turbulent in the post–Cold War era.

In this conclusion, I will briefly do three things: First, I shall synthesize the various chapters' arguments about the new economic, environmental, social, and political aspects of the post–Cold War security environment in the Caribbean. Second, I shall briefly consider whether and how this emerging set of security concerns challenges our major theoretical paradigm of international relations—realism. Finally, I shall explore the implications of these developments for U. S. foreign policy.

My bottom line is that the post–Cold War Caribbean security environment, while perhaps not more threatening than during the Cold War, will nonetheless remain unsettled. While many of these challenges will be new and different from the Cold War, realism will still tell us a lot about what this new security environment will look like. Unfortunately, the United States will find itself less, rather than more, able to deal with these new issues in the post–Cold War American Mediterranean.

THE NEW CARIBBEAN "SECURITY" ENVIRONMENT

All of the authors of this volume have embraced a more or less broad definition of "security." This is in line with the trend in recent years to include economic, environmental, social, and political problems under the rubric of "security." While there is no doubt that these all are important issues, the usefulness of calling them "security" is questionable.[2] Broadening the definition of security in recent years was the result of the desire of many scholars and practitioners to direct more attention and resources to serious problems that previously had not received adequate consideration or money. As a rhetorical device for energizing scholarly and governmental discussion of, and directing attention to, the economic, environmental, social, and political problems affecting the post–Cold War Caribbean, this broader definition of security seems reasonable. But whether this rhetorical strategy will actually lead to a concerted effort to deal with these problems is unclear. As I shall show later, I am not sure this will be sufficient to keep the United States deeply engaged in the Caribbean.

Andrés Serbin posits that globalization of production and distribution of goods and services represents the complete triumph of Western economic and cultural hegemony. This is likely to have important ramifications in the American Mediterranean. Anthony T. Bryan points out that international pressure will increasingly lead to Caribbean states embracing a more liberal set of economic policies. This international pressure will have a number of concrete implications, the most important being that it will erode the state. Conversely, Serbin suggests that this international pressure might strengthen regional organizations comprised of countries facing similar problems. James N. Rosenau concludes that globalization might empower both local as well as supranational authorities. Thus, while it is not exactly clear who will benefit from the process of economic globalization, it is certainly clear that the states of the Caribbean will face a host of challenges as they lose power and influence.[3]

Both the Bryan and the *Instituto de Altos Estudios de la Defensa Nacional* (IAEDN) chapters emphasize the environmental problems facing the Caribbean region. Not only is the Caribbean acutely vulnerable to natural disasters, such as hurricanes and man-made calamities like pollution, but the region's disproportionate dependence on tourism as a source of revenue also makes it uniquely susceptible to environmental developments (cloudy weather) that might not have much impact on other regions. Clearly, the American Mediterranean has a unique set of environmental vulnerabilities and opportunities.

The future also will witness important social developments in the region. As Jorge I. Domínguez observes, there have been long-standing social problems in the region, such as racial and religious tensions, migration, and significant "clashes of civilizations" among remnants of the Spanish, French, and British empires and the descendants of aborigines, African slaves, and East Indian immigrants. In addition, as Rosenau notes, a "skill revolution" is taking place in the region that is increasing the economic and political influence of the individual. Thus, the social fabric of the Caribbean is being rent both horizontally (the clash of civilizations) and vertically (the changing balance of the individual and society, due to the skill revolution).

Finally, domestic and international political changes are affecting the region in important ways. At the international level, Rosenau traces the bifurcation between the traditional state system and an emerging non-state system comprised of nongovernmental organizations and other transnational actors. Domínguez rightly reminds us, however, that this development is not new in the Caribbean: the formal international relations among Caribbean states have always been supplemented by the informal activities of non-state actors, from pirates to drug-lords. Indeed, Domínguez argues that "rogue states"—the product of the intersection of formal and informal Caribbean international relations—will likely represent the main security problem in the post–Cold War Caribbean. Ivelaw L. Griffith's point that geonarcotics has replaced geopolitics in the American Mediterranean nicely complements Domínguez' argument by suggesting that the international narcotics trade is likely to be one of the dominant informal sectors in future Caribbean international relations.

The most important domestic political development is the fate of democracy in the region. Bryan notes that continued democratization is uncertain because of the ongoing threats of terrorism, corruption, and domestic instability. Serbin also shows how the diminishing role of the state has crippled democratization through the weakening of its traditional political structures. As Samuel Huntington argued in his classic *Political Order in Changing Societies*, democratization without robust institutions is a recipe for disaster.[4] The key question is how to foster continued democracy in the region.

Two of the authors of this volume offer somewhat different prescriptions: Domínguez emphasizes the important role outside powers—especially the United States—have played in shaping the domestic political complexion of the region. Presumably, Domínguez would assign the United States a greater unilateral role in promoting democracy. In contrast, Richard J. Bloomfield argues that international regimes,[5] rather than states, can play an important part in protecting and fostering continued democratization in the region. Bloomfield would rely more heavily on the Organization of American States, the United Nations, or even informal regimes to encourage the spread and consolidation of democracy in the region. What is interesting, however, is that both imply that an important impetus for continued democratization is likely to come from outside the states of the region.

In sum, the new Caribbean security environment is likely to be extremely complex, comprised of a whole host of non-traditional security issues (from loss of state sovereignty to continued democratization) and peopled by a heterogeneous mix of traditional (states) and non-traditional (organized crime, multinational corporations, and transnational social movements) actors. The complex interrelationship among economic, environmental, social, and political elements in the Caribbean narcotics problem best illustrates the complicated nature of the emerging Caribbean security environment. Both Roseneau and Domínguez contend that this new security environment calls into question the analytical and practical utility of the traditional realist model of international relations. But is this really the case?

REALISM AND POST–COLD WAR CARIBBEAN INTERNATIONAL RELATIONS

The realist view of international relations rests on three core assumptions. International politics are shaped primarily by states, large states must fend for themselves because they face an anarchical international environment while smaller states do what they must because they are on the lower rungs of hierarchical regional relations, therefore international relations will frequently be conflictual.[6] At first glance, many of the developments highlighted by the authors in this book seem to challenge these assumptions. However, further reflection suggests that realism still has much to tell us about post-cold war international relations in the American Mediterranean.

Let us begin with the weakening of Caribbean states. It is true that globalization and other factors have taken their toll on these states. But the weakness of the state in the Caribbean, as in many other former colonial areas, is not new. In contrast to the strong states of the developed regions of Europe and Asia, which emerged from the crucible of war, most of the states in the Caribbean gained their independence not through sustained war but as the result of the collapse of moribund empires. The link between war and strong states is well established.[7] The link between the lack of external conflict and weaker states is also becoming apparent.[8] Many signs of state debility have long been apparent in the Caribbean. Nonetheless, it is intriguing that a number of the authors look to the intersection of the formal and informal sectors to find the key actors in post–Cold War Caribbean international relations. For example, Domínguez points to rogue states, rather than nongovernmental organizations or transnational actors, as the key threat to peace and stability in the future. While the role of the state in the Caribbean is changing, it will remain the primary actor in the international relations of the American Mediterranean.

Similarly, most of the authors of this volume do not anticipate a fundamental change in the ordering principle of Caribbean international relations. The Caribbean is not anarchic, and it never has been. Rather, for much of its history, it has been a hierarchical region under the dominance of one or more great powers. Throughout the Cold War, the dominant power was of course the United States. With the end of the Cold War, the United States may exercise less overt control of the region. As it does, the region is likely to become more anarchical. Griffith's compelling but disturbing vision of a region driven by geonarcotics suggests, to paraphrase Clausewitz, a region continuing to be ordered by the logic of realism if using the grammar of other issues.

Finally, the fact that all of the authors of this volume continue to insist on using the traditional term "security" (albeit in a somewhat non-traditional way) to characterize the problems facing the region suggests that they believe future conflict among states is not impossible. Except for Bloomfield and the IAEDN chapters, most of the other authors have a markedly restrained view of the prospects for peace and stability in the region. Even Roseneau, an arch-critic of realism, characterizes his view of post–Cold War international relations in the American Mediterranean as one of "turbulence." A turbulent Caribbean is also what realism anticipates. But is the turbulent Caribbean something in which the United States will be deeply and constructively engaged?

A U. S. FOREIGN POLICY FOR THE POST–COLD WAR CARIBBEAN?

The U. S. government acknowledges that the problems raised by the authors of this book must be addressed in large measure through concerted U. S. diplomatic efforts.[9] Former Secretary of State Warren Christopher repeatedly emphasized the importance of consolidating democracy in the region, deepening economic integration, fighting corruption, and strengthening the power of international organizations such as the OAS in order to successfully manage post-cold war Caribbean international relations.[10] That the United States is aware of the major security challenges in the post–Cold War Caribbean is clear; whether it can or will effectively meet them is less clear.

It was the conventional wisdom during the Cold War in the Western Hemisphere, and especially among many Latin Americans, that most of what was wrong with U. S. policies toward the region was the result of excessive preoccupation with U. S. national security concerns.[11] The basic argument was that this preoccupation caused the United States to overestimate the importance of regional conflicts for the global Cold War rivalry and underestimate the particular regional and domestic dynamics in these cases. While there is certainly a measure of truth in this conventional wisdom, there are nevertheless reasons for thinking that we might look back to the Cold War period of U. S. Caribbean policies with some nostalgia. While I certainly would not want to minimize the human costs of the Cold War in Latin America, I will suggest three reasons why the U. S. Cold War foreign policy was not all bad. First, during the Cold War—and the other periods of intense international security competition of this century—the Caribbean was a primary concern of U. S. foreign policy. At present, it is probably secondary or tertiary. Second, U. S. policies had a modicum of rationality and coherence during these high-threat periods, but were quite incoherent and irrational during lower-threat periods. Finally, other issues in U. S. foreign policy, such as economic, environmental, social, and political concerns have historically not produced as coherent a set of U. S. policies toward the region. There is a growing consensus among practitioners that post–Cold War U. S. foreign policy has become less rational and consistent.[12]

For example, early U. S. policy toward the Cuban Revolution was heavily influenced by economic and other non-security considerations. Castro's seizure of power adversely affected a number of significant U. S. economic interests and his vociferous nationalism and increasingly evident Leftist ideology also raised the ideological hackles in the American government. Initial U. S. policy responses were incoherent and contradictory. On the one hand, under pressure from U. S. business interests and the anti-communist right, the U. S. government opposed Cuban expropriations of U. S. economic assets and sought to stem Castro's leftward drift. On the other hand, the Eisenhower and Kennedy administrations also sought some degree of normal relations with Castro's Cuba. The fundamental inconsistency of trying to live with Castro's Cuba, while simultaneously trying to overthrow it, did not seem to have become apparent to the U. S. government until the Cuban missile crisis of 1962. The covert deployment of Soviet nuclear missiles presented the United States with a direct threat to its national security by giving the Soviet Union a robust capacity for targeting the United States with nuclear weapons. Ironically, this crisis was finally resolved when the Kennedy administration concluded that U. S. national security did not really require a capitalist and pro-American regime in Havana, but only the evacuation of Soviet nuclear missiles.[13] Once again, economic and ideological considerations produced an inconsistent and incoherent U. S. policy; national security considerations, in contrast, produced just the opposite.

What are the implications for the U. S. post–Cold War foreign policy toward the Caribbean? My guess is that if the post–Cold War international security environment remains turbulent but not directly threatening, we will again see U. S. policies toward the Caribbean that are animated primarily by economic and ideological considerations.[14] These sorts of considerations are less likely to lead to rational and consistent policies, therefore U. S. foreign policy toward the region is likely to be confused and contradictory. For example: The debate over the U. S. economic stake in the Mexican financial bailout has been quite controversial and highly ideological. The Clinton administration was ultimately forced to adopt second-best measures for financing the move and was forced to put significant conditions on its aid to Mexico.[15] The Mexican bailout controversy divided the American government and public about the wisdom of extending the benefits of the North American Free Trade Area (NAFTA) to the Caribbean.[16] A similarly bitter and contentious debate has ensued over U. S. intervention to restore democracy in Haiti.[17] And we are also in the midst of a major debate about what the U. S. post–Cold War policy should be toward Cuba.[18] The acrimonious debate over U. S. policy toward free trade in the Caribbean, and the political futures of Cuba and Haiti may be a harbinger of future U. S. Caribbean policy. In short, I predict that U. S. policy toward the region will be far less rational and coherent as long as the security environment remains turbulent but not directly threatening to the United States, therefore the United States is unlikely to play the same consistent role in the Caribbean in the post–Cold War period that it did in the recent past.[19]

In sum, if the authors of this book are correct, the post–Cold War Caribbean security environment will be quite complex. The winds of economic change will buffet Caribbean states; environmental problems, both natural and man-made, will darken the American Mediterranean's pristine waters and fresh air; social dislocations will continue to rend the fabric of Caribbean societies; and the domestic and international challenges of democratization will continue to perplex statesmen in the region and beyond. Such a turbulent regional system is not at all incompatible with the realist view of international relations. Unfortunately, the United States is as likely to view this Caribbean turbulence as a reason to steer clear rather than to try to chart a course through it. Conversely, an America fully immersed in the Caribbean might even add to its turbulence.

NOTES

1. See Michael C. Desch, *When the Third World Matters: Latin America and U. S. Grand Strategy* (Baltimore: Johns Hopkins University Press, 1993).

2. This debate is fully aired in Michael C. Desch, "Security Studies and the Social Sciences: An Agenda for the Future" (Report on a workshop held on 30 and 31 May 1991 at the University of Southern California).

3. I discuss the changing nature of the state in "War and Strong States, Peace and Weak States?" *International Organization*, vol. 50, no. 2 (spring 1996), 237–68.

4. Samuel Huntington, *Political Order in Changing Societies* (New Haven: Yale University Press, 1968).

5. The definitive discussion of regimes is Stephen Krasner, ed., *International Regimes* (Ithaca: Cornell University Press, 1983).

6. The seminal statement of modern realism remains Kenneth N. Waltz, *Theory of International Politics* (Reading, Mass.: Addison-Wesley, 1979). Excellent discussions of realism are contained in two special issues of *Security Studies*, vol. 5, nos. 2 and 3 (winter 1995 and spring 1996).

7. Otto Hintze, "Military Organization and the Organization of the State" in Felix Gilbert, ed., *The Historical Essays of Otto Hintze* (Oxford: Oxford University Press, 1975), 178–215 is the classic statement of this argument.

8. See Jeffrey Herbst, "War and the State in Africa," *International Security*, vol. 14, no. 4 (spring 1990), 117–39.

9. I develop this argument at length in "Why Latin America May Miss the Cold War" in Jorge Domínguez, ed., *Security, Peace, and Democracy in Latin America and the Caribbean: Challenges for the Post-Cold War Era* (Pittsburgh: University of Pittsburgh Press, forthcoming).

10. Secretary of State Warren Christopher, "The OAS: Playing an Essential Role in the Western Hemisphere," *U. S. Department of State Dispatch*, vol. 6, no. 24 (June 12, 1995), 491.

11. See, for example, Lars Schoultz, *National Security and United States Policy Toward Latin America* (Princeton University Press, 1987), 330; William Leogrande, "A Splendid Little War: Drawing the Line in El Salvador," *International Security*, vol. 6, no. 1 (summer 1981), 27–52; and Jerome Slater, "Dominos in Central America: Will They Fall? Does It Matter?," *International Security*, vol. 12, no. 2 (fall 1987), 105–34.

12. See, for example, Raymond Seitz, "From the Jaws of Victory," *The Economist* (May 27, 1995), 21–23.

13. Desch, *When the Third World Matters*, 89–114.

14. It is likely that U. S. policy toward Latin America will more discriminate. For example, national security concerns will still play a role in U. S. policy toward Mexico. On this see Pierre Thomas and Bradley Graham, "U. S. Drafts Plan for Influx of Illegal Immigrants," *Washington Post* (April 8, 1995), 6, and Lisa Burgess, "Bracing for an Exodus," *Journal of Commerce* (April 7, 1995), 1. In fact, Mexico does not fall under the rubric of

the U. S. Southern Command in Panama but rather under the U. S. Forces Command, which is responsible for the defense of the continental United States.

15. "To the Rescue," and "Scenes From a Border," *The Economist* (February 4, 1995), 13–14, 24–25.

16. Larry Rohter, "Free Trade Goes South With or Without U. S.," *New York Times* (January 6, 1997), 8.

17. Elaine Sciolino, "Top U. S. Officials Divided in Debate On Invading Haiti," *New York Times* (August 4, 1994), 1, 10.

18. See Steven Greenhouse, "Clinton Opposes Move to Toughen Embargo on Cuba," *New York Times* (May 5, 1995), 1, 8, and Peter Kornbluh, "From Here to Cuba," *New York Times* (May 17, 1995), 19.

19. For a similarly pessimistic argument, see Jorge Castaneda, "Latin America and the End of the Cold War: An Essay in Frustration," in Abraham F. Lowenthal and Gregory F. Treverton, eds., *Latin America in a New World* (Boulder: Westview Press, 1994), 28–52. Castaneda foresees an increase in hemispheric conflict due to "new issues" such as drugs and migration.

ABOUT THE CONTRIBUTORS

Richard J. Bloomfield is a former U. S. foreign service officer. His career included assignments as Ambassador to Ecuador and Portugal, and he was executive director of the World Peace Foundation from 1982 to 1992.

Anthony T. Bryan, Ph.D. is a professor of international relations and director of the Caribbean Studies Program at the North-South Center of the University of Miami and is a senior associate at the Center for Strategic and International Studies in Washington, D. C. His most recent book is *Distant Cousins: The Caribbean-Latin American Relationship* (North-South Center Press/Lynne Rienner Publishers, 1996).

Michael C. Desch is currently assistant director and senior research associate at the Olin Institute. He is the author of *When the Third World Matters: Latin America and U. S. Grand Strategy* (Baltimore: Johns Hopkins University Press, 1993) and *Soldier, States, and Structures: Civilian Control of the Military in a Changing Security Environment* (forthcoming).

Jorge I. Domínguez is the Clarence Dillon Professor of International Affairs and the director of the Center for International Affairs at Harvard University. His most recent book is *Democratic Transitions in Central America* (University Press of Florida).

Ivelaw L. Griffith is associate professor of political science at Florida International University and is a Caribbean specialist. He most recently authored *Caribbean Security on the Eve of the 21st Century* (National Defense University Press, 1996) and *Drugs and Security in the Caribbean* (Penn State Press, 1997).

James N. Rosenau is a university professor of International Affairs at George Washington University. His most recent book is *Along the Domestic-Foreign Frontier: Exploring Governance in a Turbulent World* (1997).

Andrés Serbin is a professor of sociology and international relations, Central University of Venezuela, special adviser to the Latin American Economic

System (SELA), and president of the Venezuelan Institute of Social and Political Studies (INVESP). His most recent book is *El ocaso de las islas. El Gran Caribe frente a los desafíos hemisféricos y globales* (Caracas: Nueva Sociedad / INVESP, 1997).

Index

airstrips, illegal, 102, 103
Americas Watch, 128
Amnesty International, 128
Anglophone Caribbean, 6, 37, 71, 83, 84, 85, 89, 90, 131
Andean Pact, 61, 69, 135
Antigua, 1, 85, 87, 104
Arias, Pres, Oscar (Costa Rica), 131
Aristide, Jean-Bertrand, 89, 108, 127
assembly industry, 65,
Assoc. of Caribbean States (ACS), vii, 6, 8, 41, 50, 61, 62, 63, 67–71, 135, 137
"authority crisis," 15, 16, 38. *See also* role of state

B-banks. *See* offshore financial havens, money laundering
Bahamas, 87, 99, 101, 103
Balaguer, President Joaquin (Dominican Republic), 89
Barbados, 1, 85, 93, 99, 104, 138
Belize, 83, 98, 101, 102, 103, 109
Bimini, 101
Bird, Jr., Vere, 87
Bogota, 99, 103
Bolivia, 44, 99
boundary disputes, vii, 2, 63, 80, 84. *See also* territorial disputes
Brazil, 99, 108, 109
British dependencies, 100
  Turks and Caicos Islands, 87, 100, 105, 112
  Anguilla, 105
  Bermuda, 100
  British Virgin Islands, 104
  Cayman Islands, 105
  Montserrat, 100

Cali, 99
Canada, 81, 82, 91, 138
Canadian-Caribbean Agreement (CARIB-CAN), 3, 63, 65
Caribbean, definition of, 11, 24, 25, 55
  geostrategic definition, 55
  ethnohistorical definition, 56
  Third World definition, 56, 62
Caribbean Basin, vii, 56, 62, 63, 67, 71, 83, 130, 138, 141
Caribbean Basin Initiative (CBI), 3, 41, 55, 56, 65, 68, 81, 83, 89
Caribbean Community (CARICOM), 41, 42, 43, 49, 50, 61, 62, 68, 69, 90, 130, 135, 137
Caribbean Development Bank, 90
Castro, Fidel, 106
Central America, 83, 84, 85
Central American Common Market (CACM), 68
  Esquipulas Agreement, 68
Central American Economic System (SIECA), 61
Cerezo, Pres. Vinicio (Guatemala), 131
Charles, Prime Minister Eugenia (Dominica), 87
civil-military relations, 127

civil society, Caribbean, 5, 58, 59, 67, 70
"civilized conduct," 90
Clinton administration, 91, 129
cocaine, 101–111
Cold War, effects of end, vii, 1, 15, 16, 20, 62, 81, 121, 122, 145
collective action, 49, 72, 88, 92, 126, 131. *See also* multilateral mechanisms
collective coercion, 125
collective interventions, 88, 89, 91, 92
collective security, 1, 9, 62, 63, 122–125, 130, 135
collective security mechanisms, 122–125, 130
Colombia, 2, 44, 46, 68, 80, 83, 84, 86–88, 98, 101, 103, 104, 106, 138
Common External Tariff, 42
Commonwealth Caribbean. *See* Anglophone Caribbean
communism as security threat, 123, 124
Contadora Group, 68, 130
contras, 86
corruption, 43, 44, 45, 64, 106, 107, 109, 112–114, 127, 137. *See also* criminal syndicates, money laundering
criminal syndicates, 8, 44, 45, 127, 134
Cuba, 2, 7, 35, 36, 62, 63, 66, 68, 81, 83, 85, 86, 87, 89, 90, 91, 105, 138, 141, 150, 151
    government involvement in drug trade, 105, 106, 107
Cuban Democracy Act (CDA), 91
Cuban Liberty and Democracy Act (CLDA), 91

defense of democracy regime, 125, 126, 129, 130
deforestation, 2, 140. *See also* environmental degradation
democracy, 35, 37, 80, 89, 90, 125–7, 129, 130, 136, 141, 147. *See also* defense-of-democracy regime
"democratic deficit," 67, 70, 72
deregulation, 61. *See also* government-business relations
development strategies, 64
Dominica, 1, 42, 85, 87, 141
Dominican Republic, 2, 7, 68, 81, 86, 88, 89, 90, 107, 138, 141
drug consumption, 97, 98, 99, 100

Drug Enforcement Agency (DEA), U.S., 104, 105, 107. *See also* under U.S anti-drug policy
drug trafficking, 2, 8, 9, 44, 45, 46, 47, 64, 80, 87, 88, 97–115, 137, 148
    air traffic, 102, 103, 107–110
    maritime traffic, 102
    methods of concealment, 110–113
    transshipment centers, 101, 105, 137
drug production, 97, 98, 99
drug seizures, 101–113
Dulles, John Foster, 124
Dutch dependencies, 100, 105
    Antilles, 105
    Aruba, 100, 105
    Bonaire, 100, 105
    Curacao, 100, 105
    Saba, 100
    St. Marten, 100

East Caribbean Central Bank, 90
Ecuador, 99
economy, Caribbean, 3, 89
economic aid, 82
Economic Commission for Latin America and the Caribbean (ECLAC), 61
economic integration, vii, 3, 40, 41, 42, 60, 90, 143
economic redistribution, 65, 66, 67
economic reforms, sociopolitical impacts, 65–67
Einaudi, Luigi, viii
El Salvador, 83, 86, 88, 89, 130
English-speaking Caribbean. *See* Anglophone Caribbean
Enterprise for the Americas Initiative (EAI), 68
environmental disaster, 4, 48
environmental degradation, vii, 2, 4, 49, 125, 139, 140, 145, 146
epidemics, 4
Esquipulas Agreement, 130
ethnic divisions, 127
European Union, 41, 60, 63, 65, 72, 81, 90, 91, 143
    Lome Convention, 41, 63, 65, 81, 90, 143
extra-regional actors, 81, 82, 83

Federation of the West Indies. *See* West Indian Federation

Fernandez, Pres. Leonel (Dominican Republic), 89
file folder banks. *See* offshore financial havens, money laundering
financial specialization, 4
"fragmegration," 7, 16, 18, 20, 26, 27
France, 2, 81, 138
France, Departements d'Outre Mer (DOMs). *See* French dependencies
free trade agreements, 40–43, 60, 67. *See also* trade liberalization
Free Trade Area of the Americas (FTAA), 40, 41, 42, 43
French dependencies, 100
　Antilles, 138
　French Guiana, 98, 99, 100, 109
fundamentalism, 134

General Agreement on Trade and Tariffs (GATT), 42, 60. *See also* free trade agreements, trade liberalization
geography, 98–115, 131
geonarcotics, 97, 98–115, 147
globalization, 22, 23, 24, 51, 57–60, 122, 129
　financial globalization, 57, 58
　sociopolitical impacts, 65
　state role in, 58–61
government-business relations, 39, 61, 66. *See also* deregulation, privatization
government-labor relations, 39
Grenada, 1, 2, 83, 85, 99, 141. *See also* U.S. interventions, New Jewel Movement
Grenadines, 1
Group of Three (Mexico, Venezuela, Colombia), 61, 62, 65, 68
Guadeloupe, 99, 105
Guatemala, 86, 89, 93, 99, 102, 123, 124, 130
　Arbenz government, 123–4
Guyana, 2, 7, 83, 84, 85, 93

Haiti, 1, 2, 7, 36, 37, 47, 86, 89, 90, 91, 93, 99, 102, 107, 108, 127, 131, 141, 151
　Cedras regime, 129
　Combined Information and Coordination Center (CICC), 108
　government involvement in drug trade, 107
　National Drug Control Directorate, 107
　National Narcotics Service (SSN), 108
　See also Aristide, Jean Bertrand

health, 4
heroin, 99–108
High Intensity Drug Trafficking Areas (HIDTAs), 104
human rights, 67, 70, 90
hurricanes, 4, 28 n6, 140

Iberoamerican Summit of Heads of Government, 91
information revolution, 57, 58
Institutional Revolutionary Party (PRI), Mexico, 66
insurgents, 80
Inter-American Development Bank, 82, 90
Inter-American Treaty of Reciprocal Assistance (Rio Treaty), 123
intergovernmental organizations (IGO), 17, 22, 89, 90
international debt regime, 90
international institutions, 92, 93
International Monetary Fund, 82, 89, 90
international norms, 80, 90, 91
international subsystem, Caribbean, 80, 82, 83, 84, 85, 89, 92
interventions, 84, 85, 88, 122–125, 129, 131, 141

Jackson, Robert H., 29 n11
James, Alan, 29 n11
Jamaica, 1, 85, 93, 101–103, 109
Jamaican Defense Force (JDF), 102, 103
Japan, 81, 82

labor unions, 39
land erosion, 2. *See also* environmental degradation
Latin American Economic System (SELA), 56, 135. *See also* economic integration
Latin American Integration Association (ALADI), 69, 135. *See also* economic integration
leadership changes, 39
liberalism, 17, 18, 20, 22–24, 27. *See also* multilateral order

marijuana, 99–109, 112
maritime jurisdiction, vii, 45
maritime demarcations, 63, 84. *See also* boundary disputes
McCaffrey, General Barry, 99

Medellin, 99, 106, 107
    cartels, 129
Mexico, 67, 68, 85, 90, 99, 102, 138
    financial bailout, 151
Miami summit, 135
migration, vii, 2, 5, 47, 48, 85, 86, 125, 127,
    128, 138, 139, 151
military hegemony, 80, 81
military interventions, 84, 85, 88, 89
military involvement in drug trade, 106,
    107, 137
money laundering, 4, 44, 45, 97, 98, 137. *See
    also* corruption, offshore financial
    havens
multilateral mechanisms, 49, 135
multilateral order, 17, 18, 20, 22–24, 27, 60.
    See also liberalism
multicentricity. *See* polycentricity
multipolarity, 63

narcotics trafficking. *See* drug trafficking
national sovereignty, 72, 131
natural disasters, 3. *See also* environmental
    disasters, hurricanes
Netherlands, 81
New Jewel Movement (Grenada), 85
Nicaragua, 2, 83, 86–90
non-governmental organizations (NGOs), 4,
    5, 19, 62, 128, 147
non-interventionist regime, 125, 126
non-state actors, 79, 80, 88, 92, 122, 147
non-state military forces, 86, 87, 88
    U.S. supported non-state military forces,
    86, 87
Noriega, General Manuel Antonio, 87
North American Free Trade Agreement
    (NAFTA), 3, 40, 41, 43, 60, 65, 68, 69,
    151. *See also* trade liberalization, free
    trade agreements

offshore financial havens, 44, 137
Operation Bahamas and the Turks and
    Caicos Island (OPBAT), 101
Organization of American States (OAS), 24,
    71, 88, 89, 90, 91, 123–6, 130, 147
    Resolution 1080 (Santiago Declaration),
    89, 90, 126
Organization of Central American States, 130
Organization of Eastern Caribbean States
    (OECS), 90

Panama, 1, 87, 90, 103, 127
    U.S. intervention, 87, 90, 127
Panama Canal, 81
Paraguay, 99
Peru, 44, 99
piracy, 79, 80, 86, 88, 92
political economy, Caribbean, 34
political parties, 38, 67, 70
polycentricity, 81, 82
preferential markets, 66, 83
privatization, 61, 64. *See also* government-
    business relations
production, restructuring of, 57, 58, 65, 122
proliferation, weapons, 134
protectionist policies, 66
Puerto Rico, 83, 90, 104, 112, 138

quasi-state military forces, 86

Reagan administration, 83, 89, 128
realism, 17, 18, 20, 21, 22, 26, 145, 147
redistributive mechanisms, 66, 67
refugees, 127, 128
regional collective action, vii
regional identity, 71, 72. *See also* Caribbean,
    definition of
regional security agenda, 63, 135. *See also*
    security, definition of
Regional Security System of the Caribbean
    (RSS), 135
regionalization, 8, 60, 61, 62, 65, 67, 68, 71,
    72
    sociopolitical impacts, 65
Rio Group, 61, 69, 135
Rio Treaty, 123
rogue states, 88
role of state, 38, 58, 59, 64–66, 147, 149. *See
    also* "authority crisis"
Roosevelt Corollary, 90
Rosenau, James, 11–28, 29 nn7–10
Russian Federation, 81

St. Lucia, 1, 42, 85
St. Vincent and the Grenadines, 1, 85, 88, 99,
    104
    Union Islands, 88
Sandinistas, 62, 87
Santiago Declaration (1991), 89, 90, 126.
    See also Organization of American
    States

security agenda, Caribbean, 63, 122, 133–142

security, definition of, vii, viii, 2, 9, 122, 125, 134, 146

security threats, 122–125, 133–142
domestic, 124

skill revolution, 15, 147

slave trade, 80

"small islandist" ideology, 82–84

smaller states/economies, 42, 43, 65, 130

smuggling, 87, 88

social movements and organizations, 67, 70

South American Common Market (MERCOSUR), 61, 69, 135

South American Free Trade Agreement (SAFTA), 69

Spanish Caribbean, 83

strategic importance, Caribbean, 63, 64

subgroupism, 18, 19, 20, 25, 27

supranational organizations. See international gov't org (IGOs)

Suriname, 7, 81, 98, 99, 108, 109, 138

technological innovation, 3, 57, 121, 122. See also information revolution

territorial disputes, vii, 2, 63, 80, 84

threat perceptions, vii

tourism industry, 48

trade liberalization, vii, 34, 35, 40–43, 62, 65. See also globalization

transnational corporations, 62

transnational organizations, 89

transnationalism, 19, 20, 26, 147

transshipment of arms, 87

Trinidad and Tobago, 48, 49, 84, 86, 88, 93, 99, 104, 109, 112, 138

Truman administration, 123

turbulence model, 15–28, 149

Turks and Caicos Islands, 87, 100

ultranationalism, 134

unemployment, 67

unilateral order, 17, 18, 20–22, 26. See also realism

unilateral coercion, 124, 125

United Kingdom, 2, 83

United Nations, 22, 88, 89, 91, 123, 147

U.N. Security Council, 1, 88, 89, 123, 130

U.S.-Caribbean relations, vii, 7, 21, 45, 46, 90, 149–151. See also Caribbean Basin Initiative

U.S.-Cuban relations, vii, 35, 36, 150, 151

U.S. anti-drug policy, 45, 104, 105, 107, 112, 124, 128, 137. See also Drug Enforcement Agency

U.S. domestic politics, 69, 128, 138

U.S. embargo on Cuba, 91, 150
Cuban Democracy Act, 91
Cuban Liberty and Democracy Act, 91

U.S.-Haiti migration agreement (1981), 91

U.S. hegemony, 82, 92, 135

U.S. immigration policy, 139

U.S. interventions, 1, 7, 21, 22, 85–90, 123, 125, 127, 129, 131, 151

U.S. military hegemony, 80, 81, 92

U.S. Maritime and Overflight Agreement, 45. See also maritime jurisdiction

U.S. Southern Command, 99

U.S.-supported non-state, military forces, 86, 87

U.S. Virgin Islands, 98, 100, 104, 105, 112

Venezuela, 2, 9, 66–68, 80, 83–86, 88, 90, 93, 99, 100, 104, 105, 108, 109, 138

West Indian Commission (WIC), 69

West Indian Federation, 83, 84

World Bank, 82, 89, 90